Icons: The 50 Most Ir   ɔ
Shaped Our world

Copyright © 2024 J.Berryman

All rights reserved. No part of this book may be reproduced, distributed, or transmitted in any form or by any means, including photocopying, recording, or other electronic or mechanical methods, without the prior written permission of the publisher, except in the case of brief quotations embodied in critical reviews and certain other noncommercial uses permitted by copyright law. For permission requests, write to the publisher at the address below.

publishing@jberryman.co.uk

Disclaimer: The information contained in this book is for general informational purposes only. While the author has endeavoured to provide accurate and up-to-date information, the author makes no representations or warranties of any kind, express or implied, about the completeness, accuracy, reliability, suitability, or availability with respect to the information, products, services, or related graphics contained in the book for any purpose. Any reliance you place on such information is therefore strictly at your own risk.

Icons: The 50 Most Influential People Who

Forward

Welcome to the ultimate cheat sheet for dazzling your friends, impressing your dates, and winning every trivia night ever. Inside these pages, you'll find the life stories of 50 rock stars of human history, each more fascinating than the last. Think of this book as your secret weapon for sounding way smarter than you actually are.

Ever wanted to drop Newton's laws of motion into a casual convo? Or maybe you'd like to toss out some Shakespearean quotes and watch jaws drop? How about schooling someone on the finer points of genetics thanks to Gregor Mendel, or wowing them with the sheer brilliance of Marie Curie? Whether you're aiming to revolutionize the next dinner party discussion or just beef up your cocktail party small talk, we've got you covered.

This isn't just a book; it's your personal time machine to rub elbows with the likes of Albert Einstein, Leonardo da Vinci, and Nikola Tesla. Imagine chilling with the Wright Brothers as they dream up powered flight, or brainstorming with Ada Lovelace about the first computer program. Picture yourself discussing the impact of civil rights with Martin Luther King Jr. or understanding the scientific breakthroughs of Rosalind Franklin. We're talking epic discoveries, mind-blowing inventions, and daring deeds that changed the world.

From the genius who figured out gravity to the trailblazer who took that first giant leap for mankind, every chapter here is a ticket to becoming the most interesting person in the room. We've got scientists who revolutionized the way we understand the universe, explorers who charted unknown territories, and innovators who pushed the boundaries of what was thought possible.

So, dive in and get ready to turbocharge your brainpower. By the time you're done, you'll have enough tidbits to outshine even the most insufferable know-it-all. It's like getting a PhD in awesomeness, minus the crippling student debt. You'll be the one dropping historical anecdotes at parties, making insightful comments in meetings, and just generally being the smartest person in any room you walk into.

Happy reading, future genius. Your journey to ultimate smartness starts now! Prepare to impress, astonish, and maybe even intimidate with your newfound knowledge. Buckle up, it's going to be a fun ride!

Icons: The 50 Most Influential People Who Shaped Our World

Forward	3
Isaac Newton	8
Albert Einstein	12
Galileo Galilei	16
Leonardo da Vinci	20
Aristotle	24
Alexander the Great	28
Confucius	32
Genghis Khan	36
Julius Caesar	40
William Shakespeare	44
Charles Darwin	49
Plato	53
Johann Gutenberg	57
Martin Luther King Jr.	60
Marie Curie	64
Thomas Edison	67
Nikola Tesla	71
Louis Pasteur	75
George Washington	79
Leonardo Fibonacci	83
Nicolaus Copernicus	86

Johannes Kepler	90
Michael Faraday	95
James Watt	99
Alexander Fleming	103
Gregor Mendel	107
Wright Brothers	111
Albert Sabin	116
Tim Berners-Lee	119
Stephen Hawking	123
Jane Goodall	127
Alan Turing	131
Nelson Mandela	136
Rosa Parks	141
Henry Ford	145
Florence Nightingale	149
Neil Armstrong	152
Catherine the Great	156
Rosalind Franklin	160
Ada Lovelace	163
Louis Braille	166
Henry Dunant	169
John Logie Baird	173
Grace Hopper	177
Katherine Johnson	181
Emmeline Pankhurst	184
Mikhail Gorbachev	187

Rachel Carson	191
Steve Jobs	194
Malala Yousafzai	198

Isaac Newton

Isaac Newton was born on 4 January 1643 in Woolsthorpe, Lincolnshire, England. His early life was marked by adversity. His father died before he was born, and his mother remarried, leaving young Isaac in the care of his grandmother. This separation had a profound effect on him, fostering a sense of independence and self-reliance. Despite his family's hopes for him to become a farmer, his academic potential was evident, and he was sent to the King's School in Grantham. Here, Newton's interest in learning blossomed, leading to his enrolment at Trinity College, Cambridge, in 1661.

At Cambridge, Newton immersed himself in the study of the works of classical philosophers and scientists. However, it was the influence of the scientific revolution, particularly the works of Galileo Galilei and Johannes Kepler, that steered his focus towards mathematics and natural philosophy. Newton's time at Cambridge was pivotal, as it was here that he began to develop his theories that would eventually revolutionise science.

In 1665, the Great Plague forced Cambridge to close, and Newton returned to Woolsthorpe. This period of isolation, often referred to as his annus mirabilis or "year of wonders," was incredibly productive. He made significant strides in mathematics, formulating the foundations of calculus, although he called it "the method of fluxions." During this time, he also conducted groundbreaking experiments with light and optics, demonstrating that white light was composed of a spectrum of colours, which he could separate using a prism. This work challenged the prevailing theories of light and colour, particularly those of René Descartes.

Newton's work on light and optics culminated in his development of the reflecting telescope, which used mirrors instead of lenses to eliminate chromatic aberration. This invention significantly improved the quality of telescopic observations and remains a crucial instrument in astronomy today. In 1672, Newton was elected a Fellow of the Royal Society, where he presented his findings on light and colour. His work received mixed reactions, leading to heated debates, particularly with Robert Hooke, a prominent scientist of the time.

Newton's contributions to mathematics were equally profound. His development of calculus, independently discovered by German mathematician Gottfried Wilhelm Leibniz, sparked a long and bitter dispute over priority and originality. Despite this controversy, calculus became a fundamental tool in physics and engineering, enabling the precise description of motion and change.

In 1684, prompted by astronomer Edmond Halley, Newton began to tackle the problem of planetary motion. This led to his formulation of the laws of motion and universal gravitation, which he published in 1687 in his seminal work, "Philosophiæ Naturalis Principia Mathematica," commonly known as the Principia. In this work, Newton articulated three laws of motion that describe the relationship between the motion of an object and the forces acting on it. He also formulated the law of universal gravitation, which posits that every particle of matter in the universe attracts every other particle with a force proportional to the product of their masses and inversely proportional to the square of the distance between them. These laws provided a comprehensive framework for understanding the mechanics of the natural world and laid the foundation for classical mechanics.

Newton's Principia not only explained the motion of celestial bodies but also offered insights into the behaviour of objects on Earth. His laws of motion and gravitation unified the physics of the heavens and the Earth under a single theoretical framework, a monumental achievement that transformed scientific thought. The Principia was met with acclaim and solidified Newton's reputation as one of the greatest scientists of his time.

In addition to his scientific work, Newton had a significant impact on academia and public life. In 1696, he was appointed Warden, and later Master, of the Royal Mint, where he implemented important reforms to combat counterfeiting and stabilise the English currency. His tenure at the Mint was marked by his meticulous and hands-on approach, reflecting his scientific rigour and attention to detail.

Newton's later years were characterised by his role as President of the Royal Society, a position he held from 1703 until his death. In this capacity, he oversaw the publication of many important scientific works and continued to influence the direction of scientific research in England. Despite his achievements, Newton's later life was not without controversy. His longstanding feud with Leibniz over the invention of calculus continued, and his disputes with other scientists, such as Hooke and John Flamsteed, the Astronomer Royal, were well-known.

Newton was also deeply interested in alchemy and theology. He devoted a significant amount of time to the study of alchemical texts and conducted numerous experiments in his quest to understand the nature of matter. Although his alchemical pursuits did not yield the transformative results he hoped for, they reflect his relentless curiosity and willingness to explore uncharted intellectual territories. In theology, Newton held unorthodox views, particularly concerning the doctrine of the Trinity, and he wrote extensively on biblical interpretation and prophecy. He believed that a rational understanding of the natural world and the divine was possible, a belief that informed much of his scientific work.

Newton never married and was known for his solitary and sometimes irascible nature. He died on 31 March 1727 and was buried in Westminster Abbey, a testament to his stature and influence. Newton's legacy is profound and far-reaching. His work laid the groundwork for many scientific advances and his methods of inquiry established the standards for scientific research. The impact of his discoveries extends beyond physics, influencing fields such as engineering, astronomy, and even philosophy.

Isaac Newton's life and achievements are a testament to the power of intellect, curiosity, and perseverance. His contributions to mathematics, physics, and astronomy have left an indelible mark on human knowledge and continue to inspire scientists and thinkers around the world. Through his relentless pursuit of understanding, Newton transformed our view of the natural world and set the stage for the scientific revolution that followed. His legacy endures not only in the scientific principles that bear his name but also in the spirit of inquiry and discovery that he championed.

Albert Einstein

Albert Einstein was born on 14 March 1879 in Ulm, in the Kingdom of Württemberg in the German Empire. His family was of Jewish descent, but not particularly religious. His father, Hermann Einstein, was a salesman and engineer, while his mother, Pauline, was a homemaker. The family moved to Munich, where Albert's father and uncle founded Elektrotechnische Fabrik J. Einstein & Cie, a company that manufactured electrical equipment based on direct current.

From a young age, Einstein exhibited a deep curiosity and fascination with the natural world. Although he didn't start speaking until a bit later than usual, his early education was marked by a profound interest in science and mathematics. His formal schooling began at the Luitpold Gymnasium in Munich. He found the rote learning methods there to be stifling and often clashed with authorities, feeling that the educational environment was too rigid and limiting.

In 1894, the Einstein family moved to Italy after the failure of Hermann's business. Albert stayed behind to finish his education but soon rejoined his family, having convinced the school to let him go by obtaining a doctor's note. He continued his education in Switzerland, attending the Swiss Federal Polytechnic in Zurich. Einstein graduated in 1900 with a diploma in teaching, but he struggled to find a teaching position. During this period, he supported himself by working as a tutor and substitute teacher.

In 1902, Einstein secured a position at the Swiss Patent Office in Bern as an examiner. This job was fortuitous, providing him with a stable income and ample free time to develop his theories. It was during his time at the Patent Office that Einstein began to make significant contributions to theoretical physics. In 1905, often referred to as his "Annus Mirabilis" or "Miracle Year," he published four groundbreaking papers in the Annalen der Physik, a leading scientific journal.

One of these papers introduced the theory of special relativity, which redefined the concepts of space and time. This theory posited that the laws of physics are the same for all non-accelerating observers and that the speed of light is constant regardless of the motion of the light source. This was a radical departure from the Newtonian mechanics that had dominated scientific thought for centuries. Einstein's famous equation, $E=mc^2$, emerged from this theory, establishing the relationship between mass and energy.

Another of his 1905 papers explained the photoelectric effect, demonstrating that light could be understood as quanta of energy, later called photons. This work provided crucial evidence for the emerging quantum theory and won Einstein the Nobel Prize in Physics in 1921. Additionally, his research on Brownian motion provided empirical evidence for the existence of atoms, which was still a contentious topic at the time.

Einstein continued to develop his ideas, and in 1915, he presented the general theory of relativity. This theory extended the principles of special relativity to include gravitation, proposing that massive objects cause a distortion in space-time, which is felt as gravity. General relativity predicted phenomena such as the bending of light by gravity and the precession of Mercury's orbit, which were later confirmed by observations, notably during the solar eclipse of 1919. These confirmations brought Einstein international fame and established him as one of the leading scientists of his time.

In 1919, Einstein's fame was further solidified when British astronomers led by Sir Arthur Eddington observed the deflection of starlight by the sun during a solar eclipse, thus confirming his general theory of relativity. This discovery was widely publicised, making Einstein a household name and cementing his status as a symbol of scientific genius.

Throughout his career, Einstein maintained a strong commitment to pacifism and humanitarianism. He was an outspoken critic of nationalism and militarism, and he used his growing influence to advocate for peace and international cooperation. However, the rise of Adolf Hitler and the Nazi party in Germany in the early 1930s posed a direct threat to Einstein and other Jewish intellectuals. In 1933, Einstein renounced his German citizenship and emigrated to the United States, where he accepted a position at the Institute for Advanced Study in Princeton, New Jersey.

While in the United States, Einstein continued his scientific work, but his focus increasingly shifted towards political and social issues. He was a vocal opponent of the Nazi regime and played a role in the American effort to develop atomic energy, despite his pacifist inclinations. In 1939, he signed a letter to President Franklin D. Roosevelt, warning that Germany might be developing an atomic bomb and urging the United States to start similar research. This letter contributed to the initiation of the Manhattan Project, although Einstein himself was not directly involved in the project.

After World War II, Einstein became an advocate for nuclear disarmament and international control of atomic energy. He also continued to support civil rights and was a member of the NAACP, working alongside W.E.B. Du Bois and other civil rights leaders. Despite his fame and the respect he commanded, Einstein often found himself at odds with political leaders and mainstream public opinion, particularly during the Red Scare and McCarthy era, when he spoke out against the persecution of suspected communists.

In his later years, Einstein's scientific work focused on unifying the forces of nature. He sought a unified field theory that would reconcile general relativity with quantum mechanics, but this goal remained elusive. Despite not achieving this grand unification, his efforts in this area underscored his enduring commitment to seeking a deeper understanding of the fundamental principles of the universe.

Einstein's personal life was complex and often marked by periods of isolation. He married Mileva Marić, a fellow student at the Polytechnic, in 1903. They had two sons, Hans Albert and Eduard, and a daughter, Lieserl, whose fate remains unknown. The marriage was troubled, and they divorced in 1919. Einstein subsequently married his cousin, Elsa Löwenthal, with whom he had a close and affectionate relationship until her death in 1936.

Throughout his life, Einstein maintained a passion for music, particularly the violin, which he found to be a source of solace and inspiration. He was known for his sense of humour and his ability to convey complex scientific ideas in simple, accessible language. Despite his celebrity, he often expressed a preference for a quiet and private life, finding joy in solitary walks and intellectual contemplation.

Einstein's contributions to science, particularly his theories of relativity and his work on quantum mechanics, have had a profound and lasting impact on our understanding of the universe. His ideas have influenced not only physics but also philosophy, art, and popular culture. He is often regarded as the quintessential genius, a symbol of intellectual prowess and human curiosity.

Albert Einstein died on 18 April 1955 in Princeton, New Jersey, leaving behind a legacy that continues to inspire and challenge scientists and thinkers around the world. His work fundamentally altered our conception of space, time, and reality, and his life serves as a testament to the power of imagination and the relentless pursuit of knowledge.

Galileo Galilei

Galileo Galilei was born on 15 February 1564 in Pisa, Italy, to Vincenzo Galilei, a renowned musician and music theorist, and Giulia Ammannati. His family was of noble lineage but not wealthy. His father hoped that Galileo would pursue a lucrative profession, so he was initially sent to the University of Pisa to study medicine. However, Galileo's interest in mathematics and natural philosophy soon overshadowed his medical studies. At the University of Pisa, Galileo began to question the accepted Aristotelian view of the natural world. His curiosity led him to study mathematics under Ostilio Ricci, who introduced him to the works of Euclid and Archimedes. These studies profoundly influenced Galileo, steering him away from medicine and towards a career in mathematics and science.

In 1589, Galileo secured a position as a lecturer in mathematics at the University of Pisa. During his tenure, he conducted experiments on motion, challenging Aristotelian physics. His famous experiment, allegedly dropping balls of different weights from the Leaning Tower of Pisa, demonstrated that objects fall at the same rate regardless of their mass, contradicting Aristotle's theories. Although this story is likely apocryphal, it underscores Galileo's commitment to empirical observation and experimentation. In 1592, Galileo moved to the University of Padua, where he taught geometry, mechanics, and astronomy. This period was highly productive for Galileo, both in terms of his academic work and his personal life. He developed a series of lectures on the shape, location, and size of Dante's Inferno, which showcased his ability to blend scientific inquiry with literary analysis. During this time, Galileo also began a relationship with Marina Gamba, with whom he had three children: Virginia, Livia, and Vincenzo.

Galileo's interest in astronomy was piqued by the invention of the telescope in the Netherlands around 1608. Although he did not invent the telescope, he significantly improved its design, increasing its magnifying power. In 1609, Galileo constructed his own telescope and began to make astronomical observations. His discoveries were revolutionary: he observed mountains and craters on the moon, the four largest moons of Jupiter, the phases of Venus, and the existence of countless stars previously invisible to the naked eye. These observations challenged the Ptolemaic model of the cosmos, which posited a geocentric universe with celestial bodies moving in perfect circles.

In 1610, Galileo published his findings in a book titled "Sidereus Nuncius" (The Starry Messenger). This work garnered him international fame and secured his position as the chief mathematician and philosopher to the Grand Duke of Tuscany, Cosimo II de' Medici. Galileo's support of the Copernican heliocentric model, which proposed that the Earth and other planets revolve around the Sun, put him at odds with the Catholic Church. At that time, the geocentric model was the prevailing view, endorsed by both the Church and most scholars. Despite the controversy, Galileo continued to advocate for the Copernican system.

In 1616, the Church formally condemned heliocentrism as heretical. Galileo was warned to abandon his support for the theory, and Copernicus's work was placed on the Church's Index of Forbidden Books. Galileo complied publicly but continued his research privately. During this period, he turned his attention to the study of tides, arguing that their regularity could be explained by the motion of the Earth. This work, although incorrect in its details, further demonstrated his commitment to the Copernican model.

Galileo's most comprehensive work, "Dialogue Concerning the Two Chief World Systems," was published in 1632. The book was structured as a dialogue between proponents of the Copernican and Ptolemaic systems. Although Galileo claimed impartiality, the arguments clearly favoured the Copernican view. This publication led to his second confrontation with the Church. In 1633, Galileo was summoned to Rome and tried by the Roman Inquisition. Found vehemently suspect of heresy, he was forced to recant his support for heliocentrism and spent the rest of his life under house arrest.

Despite his confinement, Galileo continued his scientific work. He wrote "Discourses and Mathematical Demonstrations Relating to Two New Sciences," which was smuggled out and published in Holland in 1638. This work laid the groundwork for classical mechanics, discussing the laws of motion and the principles of inertia, which would later be elaborated upon by Isaac Newton. Galileo's method of combining experimentation with mathematical analysis set a new standard for scientific inquiry.

Galileo's health deteriorated in his later years. He became blind, possibly due to cataracts and glaucoma, but continued to work with the assistance of his students and collaborators. His legacy as a pioneer of observational astronomy and the scientific method endured beyond his death on 8 January 1642. Galileo's work profoundly influenced the development of modern science. His use of the telescope revolutionised our understanding of the universe, challenging long-held beliefs and paving the way for future astronomers. His emphasis on experimentation and empirical evidence laid the foundation for the scientific method, which remains a cornerstone of scientific inquiry today.

Galileo's conflict with the Church also highlighted the tension between science and religious dogma, a theme that has resonated throughout history. His willingness to challenge authority and pursue truth despite the risk of persecution exemplifies the spirit of scientific inquiry. Galileo's contributions to physics, particularly his studies of motion and inertia, were foundational to the later work of scientists like Newton. His recognition that the laws of nature are mathematical in nature has influenced scientific thought for centuries.

In his personal life, Galileo was a devoted father, although his illegitimate children faced societal challenges. His daughters, Virginia (Sister Maria Celeste) and Livia (Sister Arcangela), entered a convent, while his son Vincenzo was legitimised and pursued a career in music. Galileo maintained a close correspondence with his daughter Maria Celeste, whose letters provide insight into his personal life and the challenges he faced.

Galileo's life was marked by a relentless pursuit of knowledge and a willingness to question established beliefs. His work in astronomy, physics, and mathematics not only advanced these fields but also transformed the way we understand our place in the universe. His legacy as a pioneering scientist and a symbol of intellectual courage continues to inspire generations of scientists and thinkers. Galileo's story is one of innovation, perseverance, and the enduring quest for truth, a testament to the power of human curiosity and the transformative impact of scientific discovery.

Leonardo da Vinci

Leonardo da Vinci was born on 15 April 1452 in the small town of Vinci, near Florence, Italy. He was the illegitimate son of Ser Piero, a notary, and a peasant woman named Caterina. Despite his illegitimate status, his father took an interest in his upbringing and ensured that he received a basic education. Leonardo's early fascination with nature and mechanics was evident, and he was apprenticed at the age of 14 to the renowned Florentine artist Andrea del Verrocchio. This apprenticeship was pivotal in Leonardo's development as it exposed him to a wide range of technical skills and artistic techniques.

In Verrocchio's workshop, Leonardo learned painting, sculpture, and the mechanical arts. He quickly surpassed his master, evident in the famous anecdote where Verrocchio allegedly vowed never to paint again after seeing Leonardo's angel in "The Baptism of Christ." By 1472, Leonardo was listed as a master in the Guild of Saint Luke, the guild of artists and doctors of medicine, but he remained with Verrocchio until 1478. During this period, Leonardo began to develop his characteristic techniques, such as the use of sfumato, a method of blending colours and tones to create a more realistic and lifelike image.

Leonardo's talents were not limited to the arts. His notebooks reveal a mind constantly exploring and inventing. These notebooks, written in his distinctive mirror script, are filled with sketches and ideas ranging from anatomy and engineering to hydrodynamics and aeronautics. His relentless curiosity and observational skills led him to study the anatomy of the human body extensively, often dissecting corpses to understand the structure and function of muscles, bones, and organs. His anatomical drawings are among the most accurate of his time, providing valuable insights into human physiology.

In the 1480s, Leonardo entered the service of Ludovico Sforza, the Duke of Milan. This move marked a significant period in his career. While in Milan, Leonardo worked on a variety of projects, from designing military fortifications and weapons to creating large-scale public works of art. One of his most famous works from this period is "The Last Supper," a mural painted in the refectory of the Convent of Santa Maria delle Grazie. This masterpiece, depicting the moment Jesus announces that one of his disciples will betray him, showcases Leonardo's mastery of perspective, composition, and human emotion.

Despite his artistic achievements, Leonardo's time in Milan was not without challenges. The mural technique he used for "The Last Supper" was experimental and began to deteriorate soon after its completion. Additionally, political turmoil led to the fall of Ludovico Sforza in 1499, forcing Leonardo to leave Milan. He spent the following years travelling and working for various patrons. During this time, he painted "The Virgin of the Rocks," another notable work that exemplifies his use of light and shadow to create depth and realism.

Leonardo returned to Florence in 1500, where he was received with great acclaim. It was during this period that he painted the "Mona Lisa," perhaps his most famous work. The identity of the woman in the painting remains a subject of speculation, but the portrait's enigmatic expression and intricate detail have captivated viewers for centuries. The "Mona Lisa" exemplifies Leonardo's skill in capturing the subtleties of human expression and his innovative use of sfumato.

In addition to his painting, Leonardo continued his scientific investigations. He conducted studies on the flow of water, the mechanics of flight, and the properties of light and shadow. His notebooks from this period are filled with designs for flying machines, studies of water vortices, and sketches of various inventions. Leonardo's insatiable curiosity and interdisciplinary approach made him a true Renaissance man, integrating art and science in a way that was unprecedented.

In 1506, Leonardo returned to Milan, which was now under French rule. He continued to work on various projects, including the equestrian statue for Francesco Sforza, which he had begun during his earlier stay. Although the statue was never completed, Leonardo's studies and designs for it are considered masterpieces of engineering and sculpture. He also worked on architectural projects and continued his anatomical studies, collaborating with the anatomist Marcantonio della Torre.

Leonardo's later years were marked by his move to Rome in 1513, where he worked for the Papal Court. Despite being in the company of other great artists like Michelangelo and Raphael, Leonardo's time in Rome was not particularly productive in terms of major works. However, he continued his scientific studies and engineering projects, including work on water systems and military defences. His innovative ideas and designs during this period further exemplify his wide-ranging intellect and creativity.

In 1516, Leonardo accepted an invitation from King Francis I of France to move to the French court. He spent the last years of his life at the Château du Clos Lucé, near the king's residence at the Château d'Amboise. Here, he was treated with great respect and honour, and he continued to work on his scientific and artistic pursuits until his death. King Francis I valued Leonardo not only for his artistic talents but also for his intellectual contributions, often engaging with him in discussions about various subjects.

Leonardo's legacy is not only defined by his masterpieces of art but also by his contributions to science and engineering. His approach to understanding the world through observation, experimentation, and detailed documentation laid the groundwork for modern scientific methods. Leonardo's notebooks, which contain thousands of pages of sketches, observations, and ideas, are a testament to his genius and his unrelenting pursuit of knowledge. These notebooks cover a wide range of topics, from the anatomy of the human body and the principles of flight to the movement of water and the nature of light and shadow.

Throughout his life, Leonardo maintained a keen interest in the natural world. His studies of plants, animals, and geological formations reveal his desire to understand the underlying principles of nature. His observations and sketches of the natural world are not only scientifically significant but also artistically beautiful, demonstrating his ability to merge science and art seamlessly.

Leonardo's interdisciplinary approach and his ability to draw connections between different fields of study set him apart from his contemporaries and have left a lasting impact on both the arts and sciences.

Leonardo da Vinci died on 2 May 1519 at the Château du Clos Lucé. He was buried in the Chapel of Saint-Hubert in the grounds of the Château d'Amboise. His death marked the end of an era, but his influence has endured for centuries. Leonardo's contributions to art, science, and engineering have inspired countless individuals and continue to be studied and admired to this day. His ability to bridge the gap between the arts and sciences, his relentless curiosity, and his innovative spirit have solidified his place as one of the greatest minds in human history. His work remains a testament to the power of creativity, observation, and the pursuit of knowledge, embodying the spirit of the Renaissance and the potential of human ingenuity.

Aristotle

Aristotle was born in 384 BCE in the small city of Stagira in northern Greece. His father, Nicomachus, was the court physician to the Macedonian king Amyntas II, which provided Aristotle with an early exposure to the Macedonian court and its influential culture. However, Aristotle was orphaned at a young age and his guardian, Proxenus of Atarneus, took care of him. At seventeen, Aristotle was sent to Athens, the intellectual hub of Greece, to pursue higher education. He joined Plato's Academy and studied there for twenty years, first as a student and then as a teacher. Plato's influence on Aristotle was profound, though Aristotle's philosophical ideas eventually diverged significantly from those of his teacher.

Upon Plato's death in 347 BCE, Aristotle left Athens. He travelled to the court of Hermias of Atarneus in Asia Minor and later married Hermias's niece, Pythias. Aristotle's years in Asia Minor were marked by extensive biological research, which laid the foundation for his later works in natural science. In 343 BCE, Aristotle was invited by Philip II of Macedon to tutor his son, Alexander the Great. Aristotle's teachings had a lasting impact on Alexander, who carried Aristotle's works with him during his conquests. Aristotle returned to Athens in 335 BCE and established his own school, the Lyceum. Unlike Plato's Academy, the Lyceum was more empirically oriented, with Aristotle and his students conducting detailed research in various fields, including biology, physics, metaphysics, politics, ethics, and aesthetics.

Aristotle's works cover a vast range of topics, reflecting his diverse interests and comprehensive approach to knowledge. In metaphysics, Aristotle challenged Plato's theory of forms, arguing instead that the reality of objects lies in their substance and form as combined entities. He proposed that all substances are composed of matter and form, and their change and movement are governed by four causes: material, formal, efficient, and final. This framework aimed to explain the nature and purpose of existence, positing that everything in the universe has a purpose or telos.

In the realm of natural sciences, Aristotle made significant contributions through his systematic observations and classifications. His biological studies involved detailed examinations of various species, and he is often credited with founding the field of zoology. Aristotle classified living organisms into hierarchical categories based on shared characteristics, a method that influenced biological classification systems for centuries. His observations on the anatomy and behaviour of animals were meticulous, and his works "History of Animals," "Parts of Animals," and "Generation of Animals" reflect his empirical approach to understanding the natural world.

Aristotle's contributions to logic and reasoning were equally groundbreaking. He developed the syllogism, a form of deductive reasoning that became the foundation of formal logic. His work "Organon" outlines his theories of logic, including the principles of identity, non-contradiction, and the excluded middle. These principles laid the groundwork for subsequent developments in logical theory and had a profound influence on the field of philosophy.

In ethics, Aristotle proposed a virtue-based approach, as articulated in his "Nicomachean Ethics." He argued that the highest good for humans is eudaimonia, often translated as "happiness" or "flourishing," which is achieved through the cultivation of virtue. According to Aristotle, virtues are habits or dispositions to act in ways that balance between extremes, known as the "Golden Mean." For instance, courage is a virtue that lies between the extremes of recklessness and cowardice. Aristotle emphasised the importance of practical wisdom, or phronesis, in making moral decisions and living a virtuous life.

Aristotle also made significant contributions to political theory. In his work "Politics," he examined various forms of government and their respective strengths and weaknesses. He advocated for a mixed government that combines elements of monarchy, aristocracy, and democracy, believing this to be the most stable and just form. Aristotle's analysis of the role of citizens and the importance of the middle class in maintaining political stability was particularly insightful. He also argued that the state exists to promote the good life for its citizens, emphasising the interdependence of individual and communal well-being.

In addition to his work in philosophy and science, Aristotle made notable contributions to the arts and literature. His "Poetics" is the earliest surviving work of literary theory, in which he analyses the elements of tragedy and epic poetry. Aristotle's examination of plot structure, character development, and catharsis has had a lasting impact on literary criticism and dramatic theory.

Aristotle's later years were marked by political turmoil. After Alexander the Great's death in 323 BCE, anti-Macedonian sentiment in Athens rose, and Aristotle, due to his connections with the Macedonian court, faced political backlash. To avoid prosecution on charges of impiety, he fled to Chalcis, on the island of Euboea, where he died in 322 BCE at the age of sixty-two.

Aristotle's legacy is vast and enduring. His works were preserved by his students and later scholars, becoming central texts in the development of Western philosophy. During the Middle Ages, Aristotle's ideas were integrated into Islamic philosophy and later into Christian scholasticism, particularly through the works of Thomas Aquinas. Aristotle's emphasis on empirical observation and systematic classification influenced the development of the scientific method during the Renaissance and beyond.

The rediscovery and translation of Aristotle's works during the Renaissance sparked renewed interest in his ideas, influencing various fields such as science, philosophy, politics, and literature. His holistic approach to knowledge, seeking to understand the underlying principles of the natural world, human behaviour, and society, continues to inspire and inform contemporary scholarship. Aristotle's interdisciplinary approach and his belief in the interconnectedness of all forms of knowledge remain relevant in modern academic and intellectual discourse.

Throughout his life, Aristotle was driven by an insatiable curiosity and a desire to understand the world in all its complexity. His ability to synthesise information from diverse fields and his commitment to empirical observation set him apart as one of the greatest thinkers in history. Aristotle's influence can be seen in the works of countless philosophers, scientists, and scholars who have built upon his ideas and methodologies. His contributions to logic, ethics, metaphysics, political theory, and the natural sciences have left an indelible mark on the intellectual landscape, shaping the course of Western thought and laying the foundation for many modern disciplines.

Aristotle's dedication to the pursuit of knowledge and his belief in the power of reason and observation continue to resonate today. His works remain a testament to the enduring quest for understanding and the importance of critical thinking and empirical inquiry. Aristotle's intellectual legacy serves as a reminder of the potential of human thought and the profound impact that one individual's contributions can have on the world. His life and achievements exemplify the spirit of inquiry and the pursuit of wisdom, qualities that remain essential in our ongoing exploration of the natural and human worlds.

Alexander the Great

Alexander the Great was born in 356 BCE in Pella, the ancient capital of Macedonia. His father, King Philip II, was a formidable ruler and military commander who had unified and strengthened Macedonia. His mother, Olympias, was a fiercely ambitious woman who claimed descent from Achilles and instilled in Alexander a sense of destiny and divine heritage. Alexander's early education was influenced by these strong parental figures, and he exhibited intelligence and ambition from a young age. When he was thirteen, his father hired the philosopher Aristotle to tutor him. Aristotle imparted to Alexander knowledge in various fields including philosophy, science, medicine, and literature. This education profoundly shaped Alexander's thinking and laid the groundwork for his future conquests and governance.

Alexander's first taste of military leadership came when he was only sixteen. Philip left him in charge of Macedonia while he campaigned against Byzantium. During his father's absence, the Thracian Maedi tribe revolted, and Alexander swiftly crushed the rebellion, founding a city named Alexandropolis. This victory marked the beginning of his reputation as a capable military leader. In 338 BCE, at the age of eighteen, Alexander played a crucial role in the Battle of Chaeronea, where Philip's army defeated a coalition of Greek city-states. Alexander's command of the cavalry was instrumental in securing the Macedonian victory. However, tensions between father and son grew, fuelled by Philip's new marriage to Cleopatra Eurydice, which threatened Alexander's succession. In 336 BCE, Philip was assassinated, and Alexander ascended to the throne. He quickly consolidated his power by eliminating potential rivals, including those who had a claim to the throne through Philip's new marriage.

With his position secure, Alexander embarked on the ambitious project of conquering the Persian Empire. In 334 BCE, he crossed the Hellespont into Asia Minor with a well-trained and disciplined army. His first major victory came at the Battle of the Granicus River, where he defeated a much larger Persian force. This victory allowed him to secure Asia Minor and demonstrated his tactical brilliance. Alexander's next significant challenge came at the Battle of Issus in 333 BCE, where he faced the Persian King Darius III. Despite being outnumbered, Alexander's superior strategy and the discipline of his troops led to a decisive victory. Darius fled the battlefield, leaving behind his family and a treasure trove of wealth. This victory significantly boosted Alexander's prestige and opened the path to the heart of the Persian Empire.

In 332 BCE, Alexander turned his attention to the city of Tyre, a strategic coastal stronghold. The siege of Tyre was one of his most challenging campaigns, lasting seven months. Alexander's engineers built a causeway to reach the island city, and after intense fighting, Tyre fell. The capture of Tyre demonstrated Alexander's determination and his ability to overcome formidable obstacles. After securing the Levant, Alexander continued his campaign into Egypt. In 331 BCE, he was welcomed as a liberator and declared himself Pharaoh. He founded the city of Alexandria, which would become a major centre of Hellenistic culture and learning. During his time in Egypt, Alexander visited the Oracle of Amun at Siwa, where he was declared the son of Zeus, further bolstering his divine status.

With Egypt under his control, Alexander set his sights on the heart of the Persian Empire. He marched his army eastward and met Darius III again at the Battle of Gaugamela in 331 BCE. This battle was a decisive encounter that determined the fate of the Persian Empire. Despite facing a much larger Persian army, Alexander's tactical genius and the discipline of his troops led to a crushing victory. Darius fled once more, and Alexander entered the Persian capitals of Babylon, Susa, and Persepolis, where he seized immense wealth and consolidated his power.

The fall of Persepolis marked the end of the Persian Empire, but Alexander's ambitions did not stop there. He pursued Darius into the eastern provinces of the empire, determined to capture him. Darius was eventually betrayed and killed by one of his own satraps, Bessus, in 330 BCE. Alexander avenged Darius's death by capturing and executing Bessus, thereby asserting his control over the entire Persian Empire. Alexander's campaign continued into Central Asia, where he faced fierce resistance from local tribes and satraps. His most challenging adversary was Spitamenes, who led a guerilla war against the Macedonian forces. Alexander's determination and military prowess eventually subdued the resistance, and he established a series of cities, many named Alexandria, to secure his hold on the region.

In 327 BCE, Alexander turned his attention to India, a region shrouded in myth and mystery to the Greeks. He crossed the Hindu Kush and entered the Punjab region, where he faced King Porus at the Battle of the Hydaspes River in 326 BCE. This battle was one of Alexander's hardest-fought victories. Despite the formidable war elephants and the bravery of Porus's troops, Alexander's strategic brilliance and the resilience of his army secured victory. Impressed by Porus's courage and leadership, Alexander allowed him to retain his kingdom as a subordinate ruler. The campaign in India expanded Alexander's empire to its greatest extent, but it also took a toll on his troops. After years of continuous campaigning, his men were exhausted and longed to return home. In 326 BCE, after reaching the Hyphasis River, his army refused to march further east. Recognising the need to preserve the loyalty and well-being of his men, Alexander reluctantly agreed to turn back.

The return journey was arduous, as Alexander led his army through the harsh desert of Gedrosia. The lack of supplies and the unforgiving terrain caused significant casualties. Despite these challenges, Alexander's leadership kept the army together, and they eventually reached the safety of more familiar territories. In 324 BCE, Alexander returned to Susa, where he attempted to consolidate his vast empire. He encouraged marriages between his Macedonian soldiers and Persian women to foster unity between the cultures. He also began plans for administrative and military reforms to integrate his diverse empire more effectively. However, his efforts to blend the Macedonian and Persian cultures were met with resistance from both his soldiers and the local populations.

In 323 BCE, Alexander moved to Babylon, where he planned further military campaigns, including an invasion of Arabia. However, he fell seriously ill and died on 10 or 11 June 323 BCE at the age of 32. The exact cause of his death remains a subject of speculation, with theories ranging from poisoning to natural causes such as typhoid fever or malaria. Alexander's death left a power vacuum that led to the fragmentation of his empire. His generals, known as the Diadochi, fought among themselves for control, eventually dividing the empire into several Hellenistic kingdoms. Despite the political fragmentation, Alexander's conquests had a lasting impact on the ancient world. His campaigns spread Greek culture and influence across a vast region, leading to the development of the Hellenistic civilisation, characterised by a blending of Greek and Eastern cultures.

Alexander the Great's legacy endures through the cities he founded, the cultural exchanges he facilitated, and the military tactics he pioneered. His life and achievements continue to captivate historians, scholars, and the general public, reflecting his enduring status as one of history's most remarkable figures. His ambition, strategic genius, and the breadth of his accomplishments have made him a symbol of military excellence and the transformative power of leadership. Alexander's story is one of unprecedented conquests and the fusion of cultures, leaving an indelible mark on the course of history.

Confucius

Confucius was born in 551 BCE in the small state of Lu, located in what is now Shandong province in northeastern China. His birth name was Kong Qiu, and he later came to be known as Kong Fuzi or Master Kong. Confucius was born into a family of noble descent, though by the time of his birth, the family had fallen on hard times. His father died when Confucius was three years old, leaving the family in poverty. Despite their financial difficulties, Confucius's mother ensured that he received a good education, instilling in him a love of learning that would shape his entire life.

From a young age, Confucius showed a keen interest in the traditional rituals and teachings of Chinese culture. He was particularly fascinated by the ancient texts and the moral principles they espoused. This early exposure to the rich cultural heritage of China deeply influenced his later philosophical teachings. As a young man, Confucius took on various jobs to support his family, including working as a shepherd, cowherd, and clerk. These early experiences provided him with a broad perspective on the lives of ordinary people, reinforcing his belief in the importance of ethical conduct and social responsibility.

Confucius married at the age of nineteen and had a son, Kong Li. Despite the demands of family life, he continued his studies and began to attract a small group of followers who were drawn to his wisdom and insight. Confucius's reputation as a learned and virtuous man grew, and he was eventually appointed to a series of minor governmental positions in the state of Lu. His time in public service allowed him to put his philosophical ideas into practice, advocating for governance based on moral principles rather than coercion.

As Confucius's influence grew, so did his frustration with the political corruption and moral decay he saw around him. He believed that the rulers of his time had strayed from the virtuous path laid out by the ancient sages and that this was the root cause of the social disorder and instability that plagued China. Confucius argued that a return to these ancient values and practices was essential for restoring harmony and order to society. He emphasised the importance of personal virtue, filial piety, and respect for tradition, advocating for a system of government based on merit and moral integrity rather than hereditary privilege.

Around the age of fifty, Confucius left his governmental post in Lu, embarking on a long period of wandering through various states in China in search of a ruler who would implement his ideas. During his travels, he encountered resistance and scepticism, but he also gained many disciples who were inspired by his teachings. Confucius spent these years refining his philosophy and spreading his message, often facing hardship and disappointment but never wavering in his commitment to his principles.

Confucius's teachings centred on the concept of ren, often translated as "benevolence" or "humaneness." He believed that ren was the fundamental virtue that should guide all human relationships and interactions. For Confucius, the cultivation of ren began with the family, where individuals learned to practice filial piety and respect for their elders. He saw the family as the basic unit of society and believed that strong, virtuous families were essential for a stable and harmonious state.

In addition to ren, Confucius emphasised the importance of li, or "ritual propriety." He believed that rituals and ceremonies played a crucial role in maintaining social order and reinforcing moral values. By observing traditional rites and customs, individuals could cultivate a sense of respect and reverence for others, fostering a spirit of harmony and cooperation. Confucius also taught the importance of zhi, or "wisdom," and yong, or "courage." He believed that true wisdom came from understanding and applying the moral principles of the ancient sages, while courage was necessary to uphold these principles in the face of adversity.

Despite his efforts, Confucius never found a ruler who was willing to fully embrace his teachings. In his later years, he returned to Lu, where he focused on teaching and compiling his thoughts and ideas. He gathered around him a group of devoted disciples who recorded his sayings and conversations, which were later compiled into a text known as the Analects. The Analects provide a comprehensive overview of Confucius's philosophy, covering topics such as ethics, politics, education, and personal conduct. They reflect his belief in the importance of moral self-cultivation and the role of virtuous leadership in creating a just and harmonious society.

Confucius's teachings also stressed the value of education and lifelong learning. He believed that anyone, regardless of social status, could achieve moral excellence through study and self-discipline. Confucius himself was a tireless learner, constantly seeking to expand his knowledge and understanding. He encouraged his disciples to question and reflect on their own actions and beliefs, fostering a spirit of critical inquiry and intellectual growth. Through his teachings, Confucius sought to cultivate virtuous individuals who would serve as moral exemplars for others. He believed that by cultivating their own character, individuals could positively influence those around them, creating a ripple effect that would ultimately lead to a more just and harmonious society.

Confucius's approach to governance was based on the idea that rulers should lead by example. He argued that a virtuous ruler, who governed with ren and li, would inspire the people to follow suit, thereby creating a stable and prosperous state. Confucius believed that the key to good governance lay in the moral character of the ruler rather than the strict enforcement of laws and punishments. He saw the role of the ruler as that of a moral guide and mentor, whose primary responsibility was to cultivate virtue in himself and his subjects.

Throughout his life, Confucius remained deeply committed to his vision of a just and harmonious society. Despite the many setbacks and challenges he faced, he never wavered in his belief in the transformative power of virtue and moral education. His dedication to his principles and his unwavering pursuit of knowledge and self-improvement continue to inspire people around the world.

Confucius died in 479 BCE at the age of seventy-two. His disciples continued to spread his teachings, and over time, Confucianism became the dominant philosophical and ethical system in China. Confucius's ideas influenced countless aspects of Chinese society, from politics and education to family life and personal conduct. His emphasis on moral self-cultivation, respect for tradition, and the importance of virtuous leadership left a lasting legacy that continues to shape Chinese culture and thought.

The enduring appeal of Confucius's teachings lies in their emphasis on universal moral principles and their practical application to everyday life. His philosophy offers a comprehensive framework for understanding human relationships and the role of virtue in creating a just and harmonious society. Confucius's insights into the nature of morality, the importance of education, and the role of the family in nurturing ethical behaviour remain relevant to contemporary discussions of ethics and social responsibility.

Confucius's life and teachings serve as a powerful reminder of the potential for individuals to effect positive change through the cultivation of virtue and the pursuit of knowledge. His legacy continues to inspire and guide people in their efforts to lead ethical lives and contribute to the well-being of their communities. As a philosopher, teacher, and moral exemplar, Confucius's impact on the world is a testament to the enduring power of wisdom and the transformative potential of ethical living.

Genghis Khan

Genghis Khan, originally named Temujin, was born around 1162 in the rugged steppes of Mongolia. He was the son of Yesugei, a minor tribal chieftain of the Borjigin clan, and Hoelun, who was kidnapped by Yesugei from her Merkit tribe husband. His early life was marked by hardship. When Temujin was about nine years old, his father was poisoned by the Tatars, leaving his family vulnerable. As a result, Temujin, his mother, and his siblings were abandoned by their clan and forced to survive on their own in the harsh Mongolian landscape. These early struggles instilled in him a resilience and determination that would later define his conquests.

Temujin's rise to power began with a series of strategic alliances and battles. He sought the support of his father's anda (blood brother) Toghrul, the khan of the Keraites, and established a close bond with Jamukha, a childhood friend. However, as Temujin's power grew, tensions with Jamukha, who also harboured ambitions of leadership, led to a bitter rivalry. In 1186, Temujin was elected khan of the Mongols, but this move provoked the jealousy of Jamukha, who attacked him with a force of 30,000 troops. Temujin was defeated and retreated, but he learned valuable lessons in warfare and leadership from this encounter.

Over the next several years, Temujin gradually consolidated power among the Mongol tribes. He demonstrated a unique ability to attract and retain followers by promoting meritocracy and loyalty over traditional tribal affiliations. He rewarded talent and loyalty, regardless of a person's background, and implemented a code of laws known as the Yassa, which helped to maintain order and discipline within his growing empire. Temujin's innovative military strategies, including the use of highly mobile cavalry and sophisticated communication networks, gave him a significant advantage over his rivals.

In 1206, after a series of victories over rival tribes and the unification of the Mongol people, Temujin was proclaimed Genghis Khan, meaning "universal ruler." This event marked the beginning of his transformation from a tribal leader to the founder of one of the largest empires in history. Genghis Khan quickly turned his attention to expanding his territory beyond Mongolia. His first major campaign outside Mongolia was against the Western Xia dynasty in northwestern China. The Western Xia were a formidable opponent, but Genghis Khan's superior tactics and relentless assaults eventually forced their surrender in 1210.

Following the subjugation of the Western Xia, Genghis Khan turned his attention to the Jin dynasty, which ruled northern China. The Jin dynasty had previously supported rival Mongol factions, making them a natural target for Genghis Khan's expansionist ambitions. In 1211, he launched a massive invasion of the Jin, utilising his trademark strategies of speed, surprise, and psychological warfare. The Mongol forces captured key cities and inflicted heavy casualties on the Jin armies. By 1215, the Mongols had captured the Jin capital of Zhongdu (modern-day Beijing), forcing the Jin rulers to retreat south.

With northern China largely under his control, Genghis Khan looked westward to the Khwarezmian Empire, which encompassed much of present-day Iran, Turkmenistan, Uzbekistan, and Kazakhstan. Relations between the Mongols and the Khwarezmians initially appeared amicable, as Genghis Khan sought to establish trade links with the prosperous region. However, the execution of a Mongol trade caravan by a Khwarezmian governor and the subsequent killing of Mongol ambassadors by the Shah of Khwarezm sparked a furious response from Genghis Khan.

In 1219, he launched a full-scale invasion of the Khwarezmian Empire. His campaign against the Khwarezmians was marked by its sheer ferocity and devastating effectiveness. The Mongol army, which included skilled siege engineers and vast numbers of cavalry, systematically destroyed Khwarezmian cities, massacring their populations and obliterating their defences. The Shah of Khwarezm fled, and by 1221, the Mongol conquest of the Khwarezmian Empire was complete.

Genghis Khan's campaigns were not solely motivated by territorial expansion but also by his desire to secure trade routes and access to resources. He established a network of trade routes known as the Silk Road, facilitating commerce and cultural exchange between the East and the West. These routes became vital arteries of trade and communication, contributing to the economic prosperity of his empire. One of the key factors behind Genghis Khan's success was his ability to adapt and innovate. He incorporated diverse groups of people into his army, including conquered soldiers and engineers, leveraging their unique skills and knowledge to enhance his military capabilities. His use of psychological warfare, intelligence networks, and efficient communication systems allowed him to outmanoeuvre and outsmart his enemies consistently.

Despite his reputation for ruthlessness in battle, Genghis Khan was also known for his tolerance and pragmatism in governance. He implemented policies that promoted religious freedom, meritocracy, and the rule of law. He sought to integrate the diverse cultures and traditions of his empire, fostering a sense of unity and loyalty among his subjects. In 1227, while leading a campaign against the Western Xia, Genghis Khan fell ill and died. The exact circumstances of his death remain unclear, but his legacy was firmly established. Before his death, he divided his empire among his four sons, ensuring the continuation of Mongol rule. His third son, Ogedei, succeeded him as the Great Khan and continued the expansion of the empire.

Under the leadership of his successors, the Mongol Empire continued to grow, eventually becoming the largest contiguous empire in history. The Mongols conquered vast territories across Asia and into Europe, spreading their influence and connecting disparate regions through trade and communication networks. The Pax Mongolica, or Mongol Peace, facilitated the exchange of goods, ideas, and technologies across the empire, contributing to a period of unprecedented cultural and economic flourishing.

Genghis Khan's impact on the world extends beyond his military conquests. His unification of the Mongol tribes and the establishment of a centralised administrative system laid the groundwork for the modern state of Mongolia. His emphasis on meritocracy and the rule of law influenced subsequent legal and administrative systems in the regions he conquered. Additionally, the legacy of his conquests had lasting effects on the cultures and societies of the territories he ruled. The exchange of knowledge and technology between East and West, facilitated by the Mongol Empire, played a crucial role in the development of the Renaissance in Europe. The introduction of new crops, technologies, and scientific knowledge from the East helped to stimulate economic and intellectual growth in the West.

Genghis Khan's life and achievements have been the subject of extensive historical and scholarly study. While he is often remembered for his military prowess and the brutality of his campaigns, it is important to recognise the complexity of his legacy. He was a visionary leader who transformed the nomadic tribes of the Mongolian steppes into a formidable and cohesive empire. His ability to inspire loyalty and to adapt to changing circumstances enabled him to overcome formidable challenges and achieve unprecedented success.

The story of Genghis Khan is one of ambition, resilience, and innovation. From his humble beginnings as a tribal outcast to his emergence as the founder of one of the greatest empires in history, his life is a testament to the power of vision and determination. His impact on the world continues to be felt, as the legacy of his conquests and the cultural exchanges they facilitated have left an indelible mark on human history.

Julius Caesar

Julius Caesar was born in 100 BCE into the patrician Julian family, a lineage that claimed descent from the goddess Venus. Despite their noble status, his family was neither wealthy nor influential during his early years. His father, Gaius Julius Caesar, governed the province of Asia, and his mother, Aurelia Cotta, was a significant influence in his life. The political landscape of Rome during Caesar's youth was tumultuous, characterised by power struggles between the optimates, who favoured the aristocracy, and the populares, who sought reforms to aid the common people. Caesar's early experiences in this volatile environment shaped his political ambitions and alliances.

At the age of sixteen, Caesar became the head of his family after his father's sudden death. In 84 BCE, he married Cornelia, the daughter of Lucius Cornelius Cinna, an influential leader of the populares. This alliance with Cinna placed Caesar in opposition to the dictator Sulla, who represented the optimates. Sulla ordered Caesar to divorce Cornelia, but he refused, demonstrating his steadfast loyalty and courage. As a result, Caesar was stripped of his inheritance and position, forcing him to flee Rome. He joined the military to escape Sulla's wrath, serving with distinction in Asia and Cilicia. His bravery and leadership earned him the prestigious Civic Crown.

After Sulla's death, Caesar returned to Rome and began his political career. He quickly gained a reputation as a skilled orator and advocate, aligning himself with influential figures like Pompey and Crassus. In 68 BCE, he was elected quaestor, the first step on the Roman political ladder, and served in Spain. Upon his return to Rome, he married Pompeia, a relative of Pompey. His charisma and political acumen won him many supporters, and he continued to rise through the political ranks. In 63 BCE, he was elected Pontifex Maximus, the chief priest of Rome, a position of significant religious and political influence.

Caesar's political ascent continued with his election as praetor in 62 BCE, followed by his appointment as governor of Spain. His military successes in

Spain increased his wealth and reputation, enabling him to repay his debts and solidify his political alliances. Upon returning to Rome in 60 BCE, he formed the First Triumvirate, an informal political alliance with Pompey and Crassus. This alliance allowed Caesar to secure the consulship in 59 BCE, where he pursued a series of popular reforms, including land redistribution for veterans and the urban poor. His tenure as consul was marked by his ability to navigate the complex political landscape, balancing the interests of his allies and rivals.

After his consulship, Caesar was appointed governor of Cisalpine Gaul, Illyricum, and Transalpine Gaul. This position provided him with the opportunity to expand Rome's territories and enhance his military reputation. From 58 to 50 BCE, Caesar embarked on a series of campaigns known as the Gallic Wars. He successfully subdued the Gallic tribes, extending Roman control over the entire region. His detailed accounts of these campaigns, recorded in "Commentarii de Bello Gallico," showcased his military genius and his ability to communicate his achievements to the Roman people.

Caesar's growing power and influence alarmed the Senate, particularly his former ally Pompey. In 49 BCE, the Senate, led by Pompey, ordered Caesar to disband his army and return to Rome as a private citizen. Refusing to comply, Caesar crossed the Rubicon River with his army, famously declaring "alea iacta est" ("the die is cast"). This act of defiance sparked a civil war between Caesar and Pompey. Caesar's swift and decisive actions led to a series of victories, culminating in the Battle of Pharsalus in 48 BCE, where he defeated Pompey's forces. Pompey fled to Egypt, where he was assassinated upon arrival.

Following his victory, Caesar pursued his opponents across the Mediterranean. In Egypt, he became embroiled in the country's dynastic struggles, allying himself with Cleopatra VII. Caesar's support helped Cleopatra secure her throne, and their alliance produced a son, Ptolemy XV, known as Caesarion. Caesar then continued his campaigns, defeating King Pharnaces II of Pontus at the Battle of Zela, where he famously declared, "Veni, vidi, vici" ("I came, I saw, I conquered"). He returned to Rome in 46 BCE, where he was appointed dictator for ten years.

As dictator, Caesar initiated a series of sweeping reforms aimed at stabilising and revitalising Rome. He restructured the debt, reformed the calendar by introducing the Julian calendar, and expanded the Senate to better represent the provinces. He also enacted laws to address social and economic issues, such as redistributing land to veterans and the poor, regulating the grain dole, and extending Roman citizenship to more provinces. His reforms demonstrated his vision for a more inclusive and centralised Roman state.

However, Caesar's accumulation of power and his title of dictator for life in 44 BCE raised concerns among many senators, who feared the end of the Republic and the establishment of a monarchy. A group of senators, led by Gaius Cassius Longinus and Marcus Junius Brutus, conspired to assassinate him. On 15 March 44 BCE, known as the Ides of March, Caesar was attacked and stabbed to death by the conspirators as he entered the Senate. His assassination marked a turning point in Roman history, leading to a power struggle that ultimately resulted in the end of the Roman Republic and the rise of the Roman Empire.

Caesar's death triggered a series of civil wars as his supporters and opponents vied for control. His adopted heir, Gaius Octavius (later Augustus), allied with Mark Antony and Marcus Lepidus to form the Second Triumvirate. This alliance defeated Caesar's assassins at the Battle of Philippi in 42 BCE. However, tensions within the Triumvirate eventually led to conflict between Octavian and Antony. Octavian emerged victorious at the Battle of Actium in 31 BCE, and in 27 BCE, he was proclaimed Augustus, the first Roman Emperor.

Julius Caesar's legacy endured long after his death. His military conquests expanded the Roman Republic's territories significantly, and his reforms laid the foundation for the transformation of Rome from a republic to an empire. His writings, particularly "Commentarii de Bello Gallico," provided invaluable insights into his military strategies and the culture of the time. Caesar's life and achievements have been the subject of countless works of literature, art, and historical analysis, cementing his status as one of history's most influential figures.

His impact on the Roman world and beyond was profound. The Julian calendar reformed the way time was measured, influencing the calendar system still in use today. His centralisation of power and efforts to address social and economic inequalities set precedents for future leaders. Despite the controversies surrounding his rule, Caesar's blend of military prowess, political acumen, and visionary reforms reshaped the course of Roman history.

Caesar's personal life was also marked by complexity and intrigue. His relationships with women, including his marriages to Cornelia, Pompeia, and Calpurnia, as well as his liaison with Cleopatra, were subjects of public fascination and political manoeuvring. His ability to inspire loyalty among his troops and to navigate the treacherous political landscape of Rome demonstrated his exceptional leadership qualities.

Throughout his life, Caesar displayed a relentless drive for power and a remarkable ability to adapt to changing circumstances. His actions, whether on the battlefield or in the Senate, were often characterised by boldness and a willingness to take risks. This audacity, combined with his strategic genius, enabled him to achieve unprecedented success.

Caesar's life was a testament to the dynamic and often turbulent nature of Roman politics and society. His rise from a relatively modest background to the pinnacle of power exemplified the potential for individual ambition and talent to shape history. His legacy continues to inspire and captivate, reminding us of the enduring impact of his extraordinary achievements.

William Shakespeare

William Shakespeare was born in Stratford-upon-Avon in April 1564, the son of John Shakespeare, a successful glover and alderman, and Mary Arden, a daughter of the gentry. He was baptised on 26 April 1564, and while the exact date of his birth is not known, it is traditionally celebrated on 23 April. Shakespeare's early years were spent in Stratford, where he likely attended the King's New School, which provided a classical education with a focus on Latin literature and rhetoric. His father's business and public positions afforded the family a comfortable living, but by the late 1570s, John Shakespeare faced financial difficulties, which likely impacted young William's prospects.

In 1582, at the age of 18, Shakespeare married Anne Hathaway, who was eight years his senior. They had three children: Susanna, and twins Hamnet and Judith. Little is known about Shakespeare's life in the years following his marriage, often referred to as the "lost years." By 1592, however, he was making a name for himself as an actor and playwright in London. Robert Greene's pamphlet "Groats-Worth of Wit" references Shakespeare, indicating he had already gained a degree of prominence in the London theatre scene. His early plays, including "Henry VI" and "Richard III," were historical dramas that established his reputation as a playwright.

Shakespeare became a member of the Lord Chamberlain's Men, later known as the King's Men, a leading acting company in London. This association provided him with a stable platform for his work and financial success. The company performed at the Theatre, and later the Globe, which became closely associated with Shakespeare's name. His works during this period include "A Midsummer Night's Dream," "The Merchant of Venice," "Much Ado About Nothing," and "As You Like It," among others. These plays showcased his versatility, blending elements of comedy, romance, and social commentary.

The late 1590s and early 1600s marked a period of prolific output and creativity for Shakespeare. His tragedies, including "Hamlet," "Othello," "King Lear," and "Macbeth," are regarded as some of the greatest works in the English language. "Hamlet," with its exploration of revenge, madness, and mortality, remains one of his most performed and studied plays. "Othello" delves into themes of jealousy, race, and betrayal, while "King Lear" examines familial conflict and the nature of power. "Macbeth" explores ambition and guilt, set against a backdrop of political intrigue and supernatural elements. These works highlight Shakespeare's deep understanding of human nature and his ability to craft complex, enduring characters.

In addition to his tragedies, Shakespeare continued to write comedies and histories. His later comedies, often referred to as "problem plays," such as "Measure for Measure" and "All's Well That Ends Well," are characterised by their darker themes and ambiguous tones. His histories, including "Henry IV" and "Henry V," portray the political machinations and personal struggles of English monarchs, blending historical fact with dramatic fiction. Shakespeare's ability to capture the complexities of political life and human emotion cemented his status as a master dramatist.

Shakespeare's sonnets, published in 1609, also contribute to his literary legacy. The 154 sonnets explore themes of love, beauty, time, and mortality, often addressing a young man, the Fair Youth, and a mysterious Dark Lady. The sonnets are celebrated for their emotional depth, intricate wordplay, and philosophical insights. They provide a glimpse into Shakespeare's inner life and his reflections on the human condition.

Throughout his career, Shakespeare maintained a strong connection to his hometown of Stratford-upon-Avon. He invested in property there, including the purchase of New Place, one of the largest houses in the town, in 1597. Despite his success in London, he remained committed to his roots, providing financial support to his family and engaging in local affairs.

The political and social landscape of Elizabethan and Jacobean England influenced Shakespeare's work. The reigns of Elizabeth I and James I saw significant changes, including the rise of the professional theatre, which became a central part of London's cultural life. Shakespeare's ability to navigate the shifting tastes and expectations of his audience, while also addressing contemporary issues, contributed to his enduring popularity. His plays often reflect the tensions and uncertainties of the times, from the religious conflicts of the Reformation to the political intrigues of the Tudor and Stuart courts.

Shakespeare's collaboration with other playwrights, such as John Fletcher, also played a role in his later works. Plays like "The Two Noble Kinsmen" and "Henry VIII" showcase his willingness to adapt and innovate, working within the collaborative nature of the Elizabethan theatre. This period also saw the construction of the Globe Theatre in 1599, a significant venue for the performance of Shakespeare's plays. The Globe became synonymous with his work, attracting large audiences and contributing to the theatrical culture of the era.

In 1613, the Globe Theatre burned down during a performance of "Henry VIII," though it was quickly rebuilt. Shakespeare's career, however, was winding down. He retired to Stratford, where he continued to write, though at a slower pace. His final plays, often classified as romances, such as "The Tempest," "Cymbeline," and "The Winter's Tale," reflect a shift towards themes of reconciliation, redemption, and the passage of time. "The Tempest," considered by many to be his farewell to the theatre, features Prospero, a magician who renounces his powers and reconciles with his enemies, mirroring Shakespeare's own departure from the stage.

Shakespeare's health declined, and he died on 23 April 1616 at the age of 52. He was buried in the chancel of Holy Trinity Church in Stratford-upon-Avon, where a monument was erected in his honour. His epitaph, reportedly written by Shakespeare himself, warns against moving his bones, a testament to his desire for a peaceful resting place. Despite his death, Shakespeare's legacy continued to grow. His works were collected and published posthumously in the First Folio of 1623, compiled by his colleagues John Heminges and Henry Condell. The First Folio preserved many of his plays that might otherwise have been lost, ensuring his enduring influence on literature and theatre.

The impact of Shakespeare's work extends far beyond his lifetime. His plays have been translated into every major language and are performed more often than those of any other playwright. His exploration of universal themes, such as love, power, ambition, and betrayal, resonates with audiences across cultures and generations. Shakespeare's ability to capture the complexities of human nature, his mastery of the English language, and his innovative use of dramatic structure have cemented his place as one of the greatest writers in history.

Shakespeare's influence can be seen in countless adaptations, interpretations, and references in literature, theatre, film, and popular culture. His characters, from Hamlet and Macbeth to Juliet and Othello, have become archetypes, embodying the range of human experience and emotion. The themes and conflicts in his plays continue to inspire writers, actors, directors, and scholars, contributing to an ever-evolving body of work that remains relevant to contemporary audiences.

The study of Shakespeare's life and works has also given rise to a rich field of academic inquiry, with scholars examining his texts from various critical perspectives, including historical, biographical, linguistic, and feminist approaches. This ongoing scholarship has deepened our understanding of his work and its significance, revealing new insights into his creative process and the cultural context in which he wrote.

Shakespeare's hometown of Stratford-upon-Avon has become a centre of pilgrimage for fans and scholars alike, with landmarks such as his birthplace, New Place, and the Royal Shakespeare Theatre attracting visitors from around the world. The annual Shakespeare Birthplace Trust and the Royal Shakespeare Company continue to celebrate his legacy through performances, exhibitions, and educational programmes, ensuring that his work remains accessible and engaging for future generations.

William Shakespeare's life and achievements stand as a testament to the enduring power of art and the written word. His ability to capture the essence of the human experience, his innovative use of language, and his profound insights into the complexities of life have left an indelible mark on literature and culture. As we continue to explore and reinterpret his works, Shakespeare's legacy lives on, a timeless reminder of the enduring power of storytelling and the universal truths that connect us all.

Charles Darwin

Charles Darwin was born on 12 February 1809 in Shrewsbury, England, into a wealthy and well-connected family. His father, Robert Darwin, was a successful physician, and his mother, Susannah Darwin, was from the influential Wedgwood family. Darwin was the fifth of six children, and his early education took place at the Shrewsbury School, where he developed an interest in natural history. He was particularly fascinated by collecting beetles, a hobby that revealed his meticulous attention to detail and his passion for observing the natural world.

In 1825, Darwin's father sent him to the University of Edinburgh to study medicine, but Darwin found the lectures dull and the sight of surgery distressing. Instead, he spent much of his time exploring the natural history collections and attending lectures on geology and zoology. During this period, he met Dr Robert Grant, a zoologist who introduced him to the ideas of transmutation of species, an early concept of evolution.

Realising that his son had no interest in becoming a doctor, Robert Darwin enrolled Charles at Christ's College, Cambridge, in 1828 to study for a Bachelor of Arts degree, intending for him to become a clergyman. At Cambridge, Darwin met influential figures such as botanist John Stevens Henslow, who became his mentor and encouraged his interest in natural science. Darwin graduated in 1831, but his path took a significant turn when Henslow recommended him for a position as a naturalist on HMS Beagle, a Royal Navy surveying ship preparing for a voyage around the world.

Darwin embarked on the Beagle voyage in December 1831, a journey that lasted nearly five years and proved to be the most formative period of his life. The Beagle sailed to South America, the Galápagos Islands, Australia, and other regions, allowing Darwin to collect a vast array of specimens and observe diverse geological formations and ecosystems. His observations on the Galápagos Islands, in particular, were crucial, as he noted that the islands' finches had distinct variations in their beak shapes, adapted to their specific environments.

Throughout the voyage, Darwin meticulously recorded his observations and collected samples, sending them back to England for further analysis. His notes and specimens provided him with a wealth of data that would later form the foundation of his theories on natural selection and evolution. The Beagle returned to England in 1836, and Darwin began to synthesise his findings, initially focusing on geology. He published "The Voyage of the Beagle" in 1839, which detailed his experiences and observations, gaining him recognition as a skilled naturalist.

Darwin's scientific work continued to evolve, and he began to formulate his theory of evolution by natural selection. Influenced by the ideas of Thomas Malthus, who wrote about population growth and competition for resources, Darwin realised that favourable traits in organisms could provide a survival advantage, allowing them to reproduce and pass on these traits to future generations. This process of natural selection, he believed, was the mechanism driving the evolution of species.

In 1839, Darwin married his cousin Emma Wedgwood, with whom he had ten children. Emma provided him with emotional support and practical assistance, managing their household and caring for their children, several of whom suffered from health problems. The Darwins settled at Down House in Kent, where Darwin conducted much of his research and wrote his groundbreaking works.

Despite his growing conviction in his theory, Darwin hesitated to publish his ideas, aware of the controversy they would provoke. The prevailing scientific and religious beliefs of the time were rooted in the idea of fixed, unchanging species created by divine intervention. However, in 1858, Darwin received a letter from Alfred Russel Wallace, a naturalist working in the Malay Archipelago, who had independently arrived at a similar theory of evolution by natural selection. This prompted Darwin to finally publish his work.

In 1859, Darwin's "On the Origin of Species" was published, presenting a comprehensive argument for evolution by natural selection. The book was a sensation, attracting both praise and criticism. Darwin meticulously laid out evidence from various fields, including geology, embryology, and biogeography, to support his theory. He addressed potential objections and highlighted the gradual nature of evolutionary change, emphasising the importance of variation and the struggle for existence in shaping the natural world.

The publication of "On the Origin of Species" marked a turning point in the history of science. It challenged established views and sparked intense debate within the scientific community and broader society. Some scientists and religious figures rejected Darwin's ideas outright, while others recognised the significance of his work and sought to integrate it with their own research. Over time, Darwin's theory of evolution gained widespread acceptance, fundamentally altering our understanding of the natural world and humanity's place within it.

Following the publication of "On the Origin of Species," Darwin continued to refine his ideas and respond to criticisms. He published several more books, including "The Descent of Man," in which he extended his theory to human evolution, arguing that humans and apes shared a common ancestor. This work further inflamed controversy, as it directly challenged the notion of human uniqueness and divine creation.

Darwin's later works also focused on various aspects of natural history and evolution. He conducted extensive research on topics such as plant reproduction, animal behaviour, and the role of worms in soil formation. His meticulous experiments and observations provided additional evidence for his theories and demonstrated his enduring commitment to understanding the complexities of the natural world.

Throughout his life, Darwin struggled with health problems, including chronic illness and bouts of depression. Despite these challenges, he remained dedicated to his scientific pursuits, corresponding with other scientists, conducting experiments, and continually refining his ideas. His extensive correspondence and collaboration with other researchers helped to advance the field of evolutionary biology and establish it as a central discipline within the natural sciences.

Darwin's contributions to science extended beyond his own research. He influenced a generation of scientists who continued to explore and expand upon his ideas. The synthesis of genetics and evolution in the early 20th century, known as the modern evolutionary synthesis, integrated Darwin's principles of natural selection with the emerging field of genetics, providing a more comprehensive understanding of how evolution operates at the genetic level.

Darwin's legacy also extends to the broader cultural and intellectual landscape. His ideas have shaped our understanding of human origins, biodiversity, and the interconnectedness of all life forms. The concept of evolution by natural selection has become a foundational principle in biology, influencing fields as diverse as medicine, anthropology, and ecology. Darwin's work has also inspired philosophical and ethical discussions about humanity's relationship with the natural world and the moral implications of our actions.

Charles Darwin died on 19 April 1882 at Down House. He was buried in Westminster Abbey, a testament to the profound impact of his contributions to science and society. Today, Darwin is celebrated as one of the most influential figures in the history of science, and his ideas continue to inspire and challenge us to explore the mysteries of life and the natural world.

Darwin's life and achievements exemplify the spirit of scientific inquiry and the pursuit of knowledge. His dedication to observation, experimentation, and critical thinking has left an enduring legacy that continues to shape our understanding of the world around us. Through his groundbreaking work on evolution and natural selection, Darwin transformed our view of life on Earth and provided a framework for understanding the dynamic processes that drive the diversity and complexity of the natural world.

Plato

Plato was born around 427 BCE in Athens, during a period of political turmoil following the Peloponnesian War. His family was aristocratic, with connections to influential figures in Athenian politics. His father, Ariston, claimed descent from the kings of Athens and Messenia, while his mother, Perictione, was related to the famous lawmaker Solon. Growing up in this environment, Plato received an extensive education, studying subjects such as philosophy, poetry, and gymnastics, which were typical for a young man of his social standing.

In his youth, Plato became a devoted follower of Socrates, whose method of dialectical questioning greatly influenced his own philosophical thinking. Socrates, known for his probing questions and commitment to seeking truth, inspired Plato to pursue philosophy as a means of understanding the world and human existence. The execution of Socrates in 399 BCE, on charges of corrupting the youth and impiety, had a profound impact on Plato. He witnessed firsthand the dangers of political life and the consequences of challenging established norms and beliefs. This event solidified his disillusionment with Athenian politics and steered him towards a life dedicated to philosophical inquiry.

Following Socrates' death, Plato left Athens and travelled extensively throughout the Mediterranean region, visiting places such as Italy, Sicily, Egypt, and Cyrene. These travels exposed him to a variety of philosophical ideas and cultural practices, broadening his intellectual horizons. During his time in Italy, he encountered the Pythagoreans, whose mathematical and metaphysical concepts greatly influenced his own philosophical system. Plato's travels also included a visit to the court of Dionysius I, the tyrant of Syracuse, where he attempted to implement his ideas of a philosopher-king, although his efforts were ultimately unsuccessful.

Upon returning to Athens, Plato founded the Academy around 387 BCE, one of the earliest institutions of higher learning in the Western world. The Academy served as a centre for philosophical and scientific research, attracting students and scholars from across Greece. It was here that Plato began to develop his own philosophical system, which he expressed through a series of dialogues, using Socrates as a central character to explore various philosophical themes.

Plato's dialogues cover a wide range of topics, including ethics, politics, metaphysics, epistemology, and education. His early dialogues, often considered Socratic, focus on ethical questions and the Socratic method of elenchus, or cross-examination. Works such as "Euthyphro," "Apology," and "Crito" reflect Socrates' commitment to seeking moral truth and challenging conventional wisdom. In these dialogues, Plato portrays Socrates' efforts to define concepts such as justice, piety, and virtue through rigorous questioning and logical analysis.

In his middle period, Plato began to articulate his own philosophical ideas more clearly, moving beyond the Socratic method to develop his theory of Forms, or Ideas. According to this theory, the physical world is a mere shadow of a higher, unchanging reality composed of abstract Forms. These Forms represent the true essence of things, such as beauty, justice, and equality, and can only be apprehended through reason and intellectual inquiry. Plato's famous allegory of the cave, presented in "The Republic," illustrates this distinction between the world of appearances and the world of Forms. In the allegory, prisoners in a cave perceive only shadows on the wall, mistaking them for reality. Only by escaping the cave and ascending to the realm of light can they perceive the true Forms and attain knowledge.

"The Republic" is one of Plato's most influential works, addressing the nature of justice, the ideal state, and the role of the philosopher in society. In this dialogue, Plato outlines his vision of a just society governed by philosopher-kings, individuals who possess both the wisdom and moral character necessary to rule. He argues that the ideal state should be structured according to a rigid class system, with the rulers, or Guardians, at the top, followed by the Auxiliaries, who are responsible for defending the state, and the Producers, who provide for the material needs of society. Plato's conception of justice involves each class performing its appropriate role in harmony with the others, guided by the wisdom of the philosopher-kings.

Plato's later dialogues, such as "Theaetetus," "Parmenides," and "Sophist," delve deeper into metaphysical and epistemological questions, exploring the nature of knowledge, reality, and language. In "Theaetetus," Plato examines different theories of knowledge, ultimately concluding that true knowledge is a form of recollection of the Forms. "Parmenides" presents a critical examination of the theory of Forms, highlighting potential difficulties and contradictions. "Sophist" explores the nature of being and non-being, as well as the relationship between language and reality.

Throughout his dialogues, Plato employs a variety of literary and philosophical techniques, using fictional settings and characters to engage readers in complex philosophical discussions. His use of dialogue allows him to present multiple perspectives on a given issue, encouraging readers to think critically and draw their own conclusions. This method reflects Plato's belief in the importance of dialectical reasoning as a means of attaining knowledge and understanding.

In addition to his contributions to philosophy, Plato was also deeply interested in the natural sciences, mathematics, and education. He believed that a rigorous education in these subjects was essential for developing the intellectual and moral virtues necessary for the pursuit of wisdom. His Academy provided a comprehensive curriculum that included studies in mathematics, astronomy, music, and physical education, as well as philosophy. Plato's emphasis on education as a means of cultivating virtue and knowledge has had a lasting impact on Western educational thought.

Plato's influence extended beyond the Academy and his immediate circle of students. His ideas were transmitted through the writings of his most famous student, Aristotle, who studied at the Academy for twenty years before founding his own school, the Lyceum. While Aristotle developed his own philosophical system that often diverged from Plato's, he continued to engage with and build upon his teacher's ideas. The debates between Platonism and Aristotelianism have shaped the course of Western philosophy for centuries.

In addition to Aristotle, Plato's works influenced a wide range of thinkers throughout history, from the Neoplatonists of late antiquity to the medieval scholastics and Renaissance humanists. His ideas on the nature of reality, knowledge, and ethics have been foundational to the development of Western thought, and his dialogues continue to be studied and interpreted by scholars and students alike.

Plato's legacy also extends to the realm of political philosophy. His vision of an ideal state governed by philosopher-kings has inspired and challenged political theorists for centuries. While some have criticised his ideas as authoritarian and impractical, others have seen in them a powerful critique of political corruption and a call for rulers to be guided by wisdom and virtue.

Despite his profound influence, Plato's life was not without controversy. His attempts to implement his political ideas in Syracuse, first with Dionysius I and later with Dionysius II, ended in failure and disillusionment. These experiences reinforced his scepticism about the possibility of achieving true justice and wisdom in the political sphere. Nevertheless, Plato remained committed to the pursuit of philosophical inquiry and the search for truth throughout his life.

Plato continued to teach and write at the Academy until his death in 347 BCE. His contributions to philosophy, education, and political thought have left an indelible mark on the history of Western civilisation. His dialogues, with their rich literary and philosophical content, remain a testament to his genius and a source of inspiration for those who seek to understand the fundamental questions of human existence. Plato's enduring legacy is a testament to the power of ideas to shape and transform the world, and his influence continues to be felt in the fields of philosophy, education, and beyond.

Johann Gutenberg

Johann Gutenberg was born around 1400 in Mainz, Germany, into an upper-class family involved in the cloth trade and the minting of coins. His father, Friele Gensfleisch zur Laden, held a position that granted the family a certain status and financial stability, which likely provided young Johann with a good education. Details about his early life remain scarce, but it is believed that he was trained as a goldsmith and metallurgist, skills that would later prove crucial in his groundbreaking invention.

During the early 15th century, Europe was experiencing a growing demand for books due to the spread of universities and an increasing literate public. The traditional method of producing books involved laborious hand-copying by scribes or the woodblock printing method, both of which were time-consuming and expensive. Gutenberg envisioned a more efficient way to meet the demand for books, which led to his development of the printing press.

Gutenberg's key innovation was the creation of movable type, individual letters and characters cast in metal that could be rearranged to form words and sentences, then reused for different pages. This was a significant improvement over the woodblock printing method, where entire pages had to be carved out of wood for each printing. Movable type allowed for faster production and greater flexibility in printing different texts. Gutenberg's expertise in metallurgy enabled him to create durable type that could withstand the pressure of the printing process without deforming.

In the early 1450s, Gutenberg began working on his printing press, combining the concept of movable type with a press mechanism similar to those used in wine-making or paper-making. This new printing method required the development of special ink that would adhere to the metal type and transfer cleanly to paper. Gutenberg formulated an oil-based ink that was both durable and capable of producing high-quality prints. His press also incorporated a system for evenly applying pressure, ensuring consistent results with each print.

To finance his project, Gutenberg entered into a partnership with Johann Fust, a wealthy financier, in 1450. Fust provided the capital necessary to set up the printing workshop, purchase materials, and cover the costs of experimentation. In return, Gutenberg agreed to repay the loan with interest, along with a share of the profits from the printing business. This partnership allowed Gutenberg to fully realise his vision and begin producing printed texts.

Gutenberg's first major project was the production of the 42-line Bible, known today as the Gutenberg Bible. This monumental task involved printing 180 copies of the Bible, each consisting of over 1,200 pages. The printing of the Bible began around 1452 and was completed by 1455. The Gutenberg Bible was a masterpiece of craftsmanship, featuring clear, readable text and intricate illustrations and decorations added by hand after printing. The quality of the Gutenberg Bible demonstrated the potential of the new printing technology and marked a turning point in the history of book production.

Despite the success of the Gutenberg Bible, Gutenberg's partnership with Fust ended in a legal dispute. Fust accused Gutenberg of misusing funds and demanded repayment of the loan. Unable to repay, Gutenberg lost the court case in 1455, and Fust seized control of the printing workshop and equipment, including the completed Bibles and the movable type. Fust continued the printing business with Peter Schoeffer, Gutenberg's former assistant, and the two went on to produce several notable works, further advancing the spread of printing technology.

Although Gutenberg faced financial ruin, he continued to work in the printing industry. He returned to Mainz and established a smaller print shop with the help of financial backers. While details of his later projects are less well-documented, it is believed that he continued to print books and other texts, contributing to the spread of printing technology in Europe. In 1465, he was recognised for his contributions by the Archbishop of Mainz, who granted him a pension and the title of Hofmann, or gentleman of the court. This recognition provided Gutenberg with some financial security in his later years.

Gutenberg's invention had far-reaching effects on society. The printing press revolutionised the production of books, making them more affordable and accessible to a broader audience. This increased the spread of knowledge and literacy, contributing to the intellectual and cultural movements of the Renaissance and the Reformation. The rapid dissemination of ideas facilitated by the printing press also played a crucial role in the Scientific Revolution and the Enlightenment, as scholars could more easily share and build upon each other's work.

The impact of Gutenberg's printing press extended beyond Europe. Printing technology spread to other parts of the world, transforming education, religion, and government. The mass production of books and pamphlets enabled the standardisation of texts and the preservation of knowledge, laying the groundwork for the modern information age. Gutenberg's invention is often regarded as one of the most important developments in human history, comparable to the invention of writing and the internet.

The precise date of Gutenberg's death is uncertain, but it is generally believed that he died in 1468 in Mainz. Although he did not achieve significant financial success during his lifetime, his contributions to the world have been recognised and celebrated in the centuries since. The legacy of Johann Gutenberg endures, and his printing press remains a symbol of human ingenuity and the transformative power of technology. His invention paved the way for the spread of information and ideas, shaping the course of history and influencing countless aspects of modern life.

Martin Luther King Jr.

Martin Luther King Jr. was born on 15 January 1929 in Atlanta, Georgia. His father, Martin Luther King Sr., was a prominent Baptist minister, and his mother, Alberta Williams King, was a schoolteacher. Growing up in a deeply segregated South, King experienced the harsh realities of racial discrimination from an early age. Despite these challenges, his parents provided a loving and supportive environment, instilling in him the values of faith, education, and social justice. King attended Booker T. Washington High School, where he excelled academically and skipped two grades, entering Morehouse College at the age of 15. At Morehouse, King was influenced by the college president, Dr. Benjamin Mays, a staunch advocate for civil rights and social change. Mays' teachings had a profound impact on King, reinforcing his desire to use religion as a force for social justice. King graduated with a degree in sociology in 1948 and went on to study at Crozer Theological Seminary in Pennsylvania, where he was elected president of his predominantly white senior class. During his time at Crozer, King was introduced to the writings of Mahatma Gandhi and the concept of nonviolent resistance, which would later become central to his activism.

After earning his Bachelor of Divinity degree from Crozer in 1951, King pursued doctoral studies in systematic theology at Boston University. There, he met Coretta Scott, a talented singer and musician studying at the New England Conservatory of Music. They married on 18 June 1953 and had four children: Yolanda, Martin Luther King III, Dexter, and Bernice. King completed his Ph.D. in 1955, and shortly thereafter, he accepted a position as pastor of the Dexter Avenue Baptist Church in Montgomery, Alabama.

King's entry into the national spotlight came in December 1955, when Rosa Parks, an African American seamstress, was arrested for refusing to give up her bus seat to a white person. This act of defiance sparked the Montgomery Bus Boycott, a mass protest against the city's segregated public transportation system. King was chosen to lead the boycott, which lasted for 381 days and resulted in a Supreme Court ruling that segregation on public buses was unconstitutional. The success of the Montgomery Bus Boycott established King as a prominent leader in the civil rights movement and demonstrated the power of nonviolent resistance.

In 1957, King, along with other civil rights activists, founded the Southern Christian Leadership Conference (SCLC), an organisation dedicated to achieving racial equality through nonviolent means. As president of the SCLC, King travelled extensively, giving speeches, organising protests, and meeting with political leaders to advocate for civil rights. His leadership and oratory skills inspired millions, and he became a symbol of hope and resilience for African Americans and supporters of justice worldwide.

King's philosophy of nonviolence was put to the test in the early 1960s as the civil rights movement faced increasing resistance and violence. In 1963, he led a campaign in Birmingham, Alabama, a city known for its brutal enforcement of segregation. The campaign included sit-ins, marches, and boycotts, all aimed at challenging the city's discriminatory practices. The Birmingham campaign attracted national attention when police used dogs, fire hoses, and clubs against peaceful protesters, including children. King was arrested and wrote his famous "Letter from Birmingham Jail," a powerful defence of civil disobedience and a call to action for people of conscience to stand against injustice.

Later that year, King played a pivotal role in organising the March on Washington for Jobs and Freedom. On 28 August 1963, more than 250,000 people gathered at the Lincoln Memorial in Washington, D.C., to demand civil and economic rights for African Americans. It was here that King delivered his iconic "I Have a Dream" speech, eloquently expressing his vision of a racially integrated and harmonious America. The speech and the march marked a high point in the civil rights movement and helped galvanise public support for civil rights legislation.

The following year, King was awarded the Nobel Peace Prize for his efforts to combat racial inequality through nonviolent resistance. At 35, he was the youngest person ever to receive the award. The recognition further solidified his status as a global leader in the fight for justice and equality. Despite the accolades, King remained focused on the ongoing struggle for civil rights and continued to push for legislative and social change.

In 1965, King and the SCLC turned their attention to voting rights, organising a series of marches from Selma to Montgomery, Alabama. The marches aimed to highlight the systematic disenfranchisement of African Americans in the South. The first march, known as "Bloody Sunday," took place on 7 March and ended in brutal violence as state troopers and local law enforcement attacked the peaceful marchers with clubs and tear gas. The shocking images of the violence galvanised national support for the civil rights movement, and a subsequent march led by King was successful in reaching Montgomery. These events contributed to the passage of the Voting Rights Act of 1965, which prohibited racial discrimination in voting.

King's activism extended beyond racial issues to include economic justice and opposition to the Vietnam War. He recognised that poverty and economic inequality were intertwined with racial discrimination and began advocating for a broader agenda of social justice. In 1967, King launched the Poor People's Campaign, aimed at addressing economic disparities and demanding better jobs, housing, and education for all Americans. His outspoken opposition to the Vietnam War, articulated in his speech "Beyond Vietnam: A Time to Break Silence," alienated some of his allies and drew criticism from political leaders, but King remained steadfast in his commitment to nonviolence and social justice.

In early 1968, King travelled to Memphis, Tennessee, to support striking sanitation workers who were demanding better wages and working conditions. He saw the strike as part of the broader struggle for economic justice and planned to lead a march in solidarity with the workers. On 3 April, he delivered his final speech, "I've Been to the Mountaintop," in which he reflected on the progress of the civil rights movement and expressed a premonition of his own death.

The following evening, on 4 April 1968, King was fatally shot while standing on the balcony of the Lorraine Motel in Memphis. His assassination sent shockwaves through the nation and the world, sparking riots in cities across the United States and a period of mourning for the loss of a visionary leader. King's funeral, held on 9 April, was attended by thousands of mourners, and his legacy was honoured by numerous tributes and memorials.

King's impact on the civil rights movement and American society was profound. His leadership and advocacy helped dismantle institutionalised segregation and secure significant legal protections for African Americans. The Civil Rights Act of 1964 and the Voting Rights Act of 1965 were landmark achievements that transformed the social and political landscape of the United States. King's unwavering commitment to nonviolence and his eloquent articulation of the principles of justice and equality inspired generations of activists and continue to resonate today.

King's legacy is commemorated annually on Martin Luther King Jr. Day, a federal holiday in the United States, as well as through numerous streets, schools, and institutions named in his honour. His writings, speeches, and teachings remain a vital part of the discourse on civil rights and social justice, offering a blueprint for peaceful resistance and transformative change. Through his life and work, Martin Luther King Jr. demonstrated the power of courage, compassion, and unwavering dedication to the pursuit of justice, leaving an indelible mark on history and the ongoing struggle for human rights.

Marie Curie

Marie Curie, born Maria Skłodowska on 7 November 1867 in Warsaw, Poland, was the youngest of five children in a family of educators. Her father, Władysław Skłodowski, was a teacher of mathematics and physics, and her mother, Bronisława, ran a prestigious boarding school for girls. Despite their dedication to education, the family struggled financially, especially after Bronisława died of tuberculosis when Marie was ten. Marie excelled academically, but opportunities for women in Poland were limited. She attended a clandestine university known as the Flying University, which offered courses to women in defiance of Russian authorities. To support her sister Bronisława's medical studies in Paris, Marie worked as a governess, enduring long hours and meagre pay. Eventually, Bronisława reciprocated, enabling Marie to pursue her own education in Paris.

In 1891, at the age of 24, Marie moved to Paris and enrolled at the Sorbonne, where she studied physics, chemistry, and mathematics. Despite facing language barriers and financial difficulties, she graduated at the top of her class in physics in 1893 and earned a second degree in mathematics in 1894. During this period, she met Pierre Curie, a physicist who was already well known for his work on crystals and magnetism. They shared a passion for science and married in 1895. Their partnership was both personal and professional, with Marie adopting the name Marie Curie.

Marie Curie's early research focused on the magnetic properties of different steels. In 1897, she began investigating the mysterious radiation discovered by Henri Becquerel in uranium. Using an electrometer designed by Pierre and his brother Jacques, Marie measured the weak electric currents emanating from uranium compounds, discovering that the radiation was constant, irrespective of the compound's state or form. She hypothesised that the radiation was an atomic property of uranium itself. Intrigued, Marie expanded her research to include other elements. In 1898, she discovered that thorium also emitted similar radiation. She coined the term "radioactivity" to describe this phenomenon.

To isolate the unknown substances responsible for this radioactivity, Marie and Pierre processed tons of pitchblende, a uranium-rich mineral. Their arduous work led to the discovery of two new elements: polonium, named after Marie's homeland, and radium. In 1903, Marie Curie became the first woman in France to earn a doctorate in physics for her thesis on radioactive substances. That same year, she, Pierre, and Becquerel were awarded the Nobel Prize in Physics for their combined work on radioactivity. Marie was the first woman to receive this honour.

Despite the accolades, the Curies lived modestly, prioritising their research over personal wealth. In 1904, Pierre was appointed to the chair of physics at the Sorbonne, and Marie was given a laboratory position. They continued their research, further investigating the properties of radium and its medical applications. Tragically, in 1906, Pierre was killed in a street accident, leaving Marie devastated. Nevertheless, she resolved to continue their work, taking over Pierre's position at the Sorbonne. In 1908, she became the first female professor at the university.

Marie Curie's subsequent research focused on the chemical properties of radium, leading to its isolation as a pure metal in 1910. She published a comprehensive treatise on radioactivity, cementing her reputation as a leading scientist. In 1911, she was awarded a second Nobel Prize, this time in Chemistry, for her discovery of polonium and radium and her investigation of their properties. This made her the first person to win Nobel Prizes in two different scientific fields.

During World War I, Curie recognised the potential of X-rays for medical use in treating wounded soldiers. She developed mobile radiography units, known as "Little Curies," and trained women to operate them. These units were deployed to the front lines, significantly improving the treatment of battlefield injuries. Curie also promoted the use of radium for cancer therapy, pioneering the field of radiotherapy. After the war, Curie continued her research, despite facing significant health problems likely caused by prolonged exposure to radiation. In 1921, she embarked on a tour of the United States to raise funds for her Radium Institute in Paris. The tour, organised by journalist Marie Mattingly Meloney, was a success, with Curie receiving a gram of radium as a gift from American women.

Curie's contributions extended beyond her research. She advocated for scientific collaboration and education, serving as a mentor to many young scientists, including her daughter Irène, who would go on to win a Nobel Prize herself. Marie Curie's legacy is reflected in numerous institutions and awards named in her honour, including the Curie Institutes in Paris and Warsaw. Despite her achievements, Curie faced significant challenges and discrimination as a woman in science. She remained dedicated to her work, driven by a profound belief in the value of scientific discovery for the betterment of humanity.

Marie Curie died on 4 July 1934, from aplastic anaemia, a condition likely caused by her prolonged exposure to high levels of radiation. She was buried alongside Pierre in the Sceaux cemetery, and in 1995, their remains were transferred to the Panthéon in Paris, honouring their contributions to science and humanity. Marie Curie's pioneering research on radioactivity revolutionised the field of physics and chemistry, paving the way for numerous advancements in science and medicine. Her dedication, perseverance, and groundbreaking discoveries have left an enduring legacy, inspiring generations of scientists and shaping the course of modern science.

Thomas Edison

Thomas Edison was born on 11 February 1847 in Milan, Ohio, the youngest of seven children. His father, Samuel Edison Jr., was an exiled political activist from Canada, and his mother, Nancy Elliott Edison, was a schoolteacher. Edison's family moved to Port Huron, Michigan, when he was seven. As a child, Edison was curious and inventive but also prone to distraction and restlessness. His formal education was brief, and he attended school only for a few months before his mother decided to teach him at home. She encouraged his natural curiosity, allowing him to read widely and conduct experiments.

At the age of twelve, Edison began working as a newsboy on the Grand Trunk Railroad, selling newspapers and candy to passengers. This job gave him the opportunity to learn about telegraphy, a skill that would prove crucial in his later career. He set up a small laboratory in a baggage car, where he conducted experiments during his free time. In 1862, at the age of fifteen, Edison saved a three-year-old from being struck by a runaway train. The child's father, a telegraph operator, was so grateful that he taught Edison how to operate the telegraph. This skill allowed Edison to secure various telegraphy jobs across the Midwest, where he continued to experiment and invent.

Edison's first significant invention was an improved stock ticker, the Universal Stock Printer, which he patented in 1869. He sold the rights to this invention for $40,000, a substantial sum at the time. With this money, he set up a laboratory and manufacturing facility in Newark, New Jersey. It was here that Edison began his lifelong pursuit of invention and innovation. He quickly made a name for himself with a series of successful inventions, including an improved telegraph system that could send multiple messages over the same wire simultaneously.

In 1876, Edison moved his operations to Menlo Park, New Jersey, where he established an industrial research laboratory. This facility was the first of its kind and marked a significant shift in the way scientific research and development were conducted. Edison's Menlo Park laboratory became known as the "invention factory," where he and his team of skilled workers and scientists worked on multiple projects simultaneously. One of Edison's most significant inventions during this period was the phonograph, developed in 1877. The phonograph was the first device capable of recording and reproducing sound, and it brought Edison international fame.

Edison's most famous invention, however, was the practical incandescent light bulb. Although he did not invent the first electric light, his version was the first to be practical for widespread use. Edison's light bulb was more durable and produced a more consistent light than earlier versions. After several years of experimentation, he developed a carbon filament that could burn for up to 1,200 hours. In 1879, he publicly demonstrated his incandescent light bulb, which was a significant breakthrough in the development of electric lighting.

To support his electric light system, Edison developed an entire electrical distribution network. He founded the Edison Electric Light Company in 1880 and began building the first electrical power station in Lower Manhattan. In 1882, the Pearl Street Station became the world's first central power plant, providing electricity to 59 customers in New York City. This marked the beginning of the modern electrical age and revolutionised the way people lived and worked.

Edison's work in electricity extended beyond lighting. He also developed the electric generator, the electric meter, and the electrical grid system. His contributions to the development of electricity were instrumental in making it a viable and widespread source of power. Edison's inventions and innovations in this field had a profound impact on society, transforming industries and improving the quality of life for millions of people.

In addition to his work in electricity, Edison made significant contributions to other fields. He invented the mimeograph, an early duplicating machine, and the fluoroscope, a device used to view X-rays. Edison's interest in motion pictures led to the development of the kinetoscope, an early motion picture viewing device, and the kinetograph, a motion picture camera. These inventions laid the groundwork for the modern film industry.

Despite his many successes, Edison's career was not without failures and setbacks. He invested heavily in projects that ultimately proved unsuccessful, such as his attempt to mine iron ore in New Jersey and his development of a talking doll. Edison's competitive nature also led to conflicts with other inventors, most notably Nikola Tesla and George Westinghouse. The rivalry between Edison and Tesla, known as the "War of Currents," was a significant chapter in the history of electricity. Edison advocated for direct current (DC) as the standard for electrical power distribution, while Tesla and Westinghouse promoted alternating current (AC). Although AC ultimately became the standard, Edison's contributions to the development of electrical systems were foundational and enduring.

Edison's work ethic and dedication to invention were legendary. He often worked long hours in his laboratory, driven by a relentless curiosity and a desire to improve the world through technology. He held over 1,000 patents, making him one of the most prolific inventors in history. Edison's approach to invention was methodical and experimental, characterised by trial and error and a willingness to learn from failure.

In 1887, Edison moved his laboratory to West Orange, New Jersey, where he continued to work on new inventions and improvements to existing technologies. The West Orange laboratory was larger and better equipped than Menlo Park, and it became the centre of Edison's research and development activities for the rest of his life. Here, he developed the alkaline storage battery, which found applications in automobiles and industrial uses. He also continued to refine his phonograph and motion picture technologies.

Edison's personal life was marked by both happiness and tragedy. He married Mary Stilwell in 1871, and they had three children: Marion, Thomas Jr., and William. Mary died in 1884, and Edison remarried two years later to Mina Miller, the daughter of a prominent inventor and industrialist. Edison and Mina had three more children: Madeleine, Charles, and Theodore. Despite his demanding work schedule, Edison remained close to his family, and his children often visited him in the laboratory.

Edison's achievements earned him numerous awards and honours throughout his life. He was recognised by governments, scientific organisations, and universities around the world. In 1928, he received the Congressional Gold Medal for his contributions to the development of technology and industry. Edison was also a founding member of the National Academy of Sciences and received honorary degrees from several prestigious institutions.

In his later years, Edison's health began to decline, but he remained active and continued to work on new projects. He was involved in the development of synthetic rubber during World War I, as part of the effort to address shortages caused by the war. Edison's research in this area contributed to the development of new materials and processes that would be important in the post-war period.

Thomas Edison died on 18 October 1931, at the age of 84, at his home in West Orange. His death was widely mourned, and tributes poured in from around the world. Edison's impact on modern society was profound and far-reaching. His inventions and innovations transformed industries, improved the quality of life for millions of people, and laid the foundation for many of the technologies that define the modern world.

Edison's legacy is preserved in numerous ways. His laboratories in Menlo Park and West Orange are now museums, dedicated to showcasing his work and educating the public about his contributions to science and technology. The annual Edison Awards, which recognise innovation and excellence in the development of new products and services, are named in his honour. Edison's life and achievements continue to inspire inventors, scientists, and entrepreneurs, reminding us of the power of creativity, perseverance, and innovation.

Nikola Tesla

Nikola Tesla was born on 10 July 1856 in Smiljan, part of the Austrian Empire, now in Croatia. His father, Milutin Tesla, was a Serbian Orthodox priest and writer, while his mother, Georgina Đuka Tesla, was a talented inventor of household appliances. Tesla credited his mother's inventive nature and his father's dedication to education as significant influences on his own intellectual development. He showed remarkable aptitude for mathematics and physics from a young age, often performing complex calculations in his head. Tesla attended the Polytechnic School in Graz, Austria, and later the University of Prague, although it is uncertain if he graduated. During his studies, he became fascinated with electricity, driven by a desire to understand the principles behind electric motors and generators.

In 1881, Tesla moved to Budapest to work for the Budapest Telephone Exchange, where he devised improvements to the telephone system and created one of the earliest loudspeakers. It was in Budapest that he first conceptualised the rotating magnetic field, a principle that would become the foundation of his later work on alternating current (AC) systems. In 1882, Tesla moved to Paris to work for the Continental Edison Company, designing and improving electrical equipment. His skills and innovative ideas quickly caught the attention of his superiors, leading to a recommendation that he work directly for Thomas Edison in the United States.

Tesla arrived in New York in 1884 with a letter of introduction to Edison, who hired him to work on improving his direct current (DC) generators. Despite their mutual respect, Tesla and Edison had differing views on electrical power. Edison favoured direct current, while Tesla believed alternating current was more efficient for long-distance transmission. This fundamental disagreement led Tesla to leave Edison's company after only a year. After a difficult period working as a manual labourer to fund his own experiments, Tesla developed an induction motor that ran on alternating current. In 1887, he filed for patents for his AC motors and power systems, catching the attention of George

Westinghouse, a prominent industrialist seeking to develop an AC power network.

Westinghouse purchased Tesla's patents, providing him with funding and a laboratory to continue his research. The partnership between Tesla and Westinghouse sparked the "War of Currents," a fierce competition with Edison over the preferred method of electrical power distribution. Tesla's AC system eventually proved superior for its ability to efficiently transmit electricity over long distances, leading to its widespread adoption. In 1893, Tesla and Westinghouse demonstrated the safety and efficacy of AC power at the World's Columbian Exposition in Chicago, cementing Tesla's reputation as a leading inventor in the field of electrical engineering.

Tesla's work on AC power laid the foundation for many modern electrical systems. He continued to innovate, developing technologies such as the Tesla coil, a high-voltage transformer used in radio technology and various electrical devices. Tesla's inventions extended beyond electrical engineering. He conducted experiments in wireless transmission of energy, envisioning a world where power could be transmitted without wires. In 1899, he moved to Colorado Springs, where he built a large experimental station to pursue his wireless energy projects. There, he conducted experiments with high-voltage electricity and wireless transmission, achieving remarkable results. Tesla claimed to have transmitted electrical energy over long distances without wires, demonstrating the potential for wireless power transmission.

In 1900, with funding from financier J.P. Morgan, Tesla began construction of Wardenclyffe Tower on Long Island, a massive wireless transmission station designed to broadcast electrical power and communications across the globe. However, financial difficulties and scepticism from investors led to the project's abandonment in 1906. Despite this setback, Tesla's vision of wireless energy transmission continued to influence future technologies. Tesla's later years were marked by financial instability and a series of unsuccessful projects. He continued to develop new ideas and inventions, but many of his concepts were too advanced for the technology of the time. His work on particle beam weapons, remote control, and advanced energy systems remained largely theoretical.

Despite his financial difficulties, Tesla's contributions to science and technology were widely recognised. In 1917, he was awarded the Edison Medal, the most prestigious honour given by the American Institute of Electrical Engineers, acknowledging his revolutionary work in electrical engineering. Tesla's personal life was characterised by eccentricity and solitude. He never married, dedicating his life entirely to his work. He was known for his meticulous routines and a deep fear of germs. Tesla's brilliance and innovative spirit often set him apart from his contemporaries, leading to both admiration and isolation.

In the 1930s, Tesla lived in relative obscurity, residing in a New York hotel and continuing to work on his inventions. He spent his final years feeding pigeons in Bryant Park, a solitary figure far removed from the heights of his earlier fame. Nikola Tesla died on 7 January 1943 at the age of 86 in his hotel room. His death marked the end of an era, but his legacy endured through the countless inventions and ideas he left behind.

Tesla's contributions to the field of electrical engineering are immeasurable. His development of alternating current systems revolutionised the way electricity is generated and distributed, making long-distance power transmission possible and practical. The Tesla coil remains a fundamental component in various technologies, from radio to medical devices. His pioneering work in wireless communication laid the groundwork for modern wireless technologies, including radio, television, and mobile communications. Tesla's vision of wireless energy transmission, though not realised in his lifetime, continues to inspire research and development in the field of wireless power.

Tesla's influence extends beyond his technical achievements. He embodied the spirit of innovation and the pursuit of knowledge, driven by a relentless curiosity and a desire to improve the world through technology. His ideas and inventions have left an indelible mark on the modern world, shaping the development of countless technologies that define contemporary life.

Nikola Tesla's story is one of brilliance and perseverance, a testament to the power of imagination and the enduring impact of visionary thinking. His life and work continue to inspire scientists, engineers, and inventors, reminding us of the boundless possibilities of human ingenuity and the transformative power of technological innovation.

Louis Pasteur

Louis Pasteur was born on 27 December 1822 in Dole, France, into a modest family. His father, Jean-Joseph Pasteur, was a tanner and a veteran of the Napoleonic wars, and his mother, Jeanne-Etiennette Roqui, supported the family with great dedication. Pasteur was not initially an exceptional student but showed a keen interest in the natural sciences. He attended secondary school in Besançon, where he earned his Bachelor of Letters degree in 1840, followed by a Bachelor of Science degree in 1842. His academic potential was recognised by his teachers, who encouraged him to pursue higher education in Paris.

In 1843, Pasteur was admitted to the prestigious École Normale Supérieure in Paris, where he studied physics and chemistry. He earned his Master of Science degree in 1845 and a doctorate in 1847. His early research focused on the study of crystals, specifically the optical properties of tartaric acid and its isomers. Through meticulous experimentation, Pasteur discovered that tartaric acid crystals could rotate plane-polarised light in different directions. He determined that this property was due to the asymmetric molecular structure of the crystals, laying the groundwork for the field of stereochemistry.

Pasteur's work on crystals earned him a reputation as a promising young scientist, and he was appointed as a professor of chemistry at the University of Strasbourg in 1848. There, he met and married Marie Laurent, the daughter of the university's rector. The couple had five children, though only two survived to adulthood. Marie's support was instrumental in Pasteur's scientific pursuits, providing him with stability and encouragement

In the mid-1850s, Pasteur shifted his focus to the study of fermentation, a process crucial to the brewing and wine-making industries. At the time, the prevailing belief was that fermentation was a purely chemical process. Pasteur's experiments demonstrated that fermentation was actually a biological process carried out by living microorganisms. He showed that different types of microorganisms were responsible for different types of fermentation, such as yeast producing alcohol in beer and wine, and bacteria producing lactic acid in sour milk.

Pasteur's discoveries in fermentation had significant practical implications, particularly for the wine industry in France, which was plagued by problems of spoilage. In 1864, he developed a method to prevent spoilage by heating wine to a specific temperature for a set period, killing the harmful microorganisms without affecting the wine's flavour. This process, known as pasteurisation, was later applied to other food and beverage products, revolutionising food safety and preservation.

Pasteur's work on fermentation also led him to challenge the theory of spontaneous generation, which held that living organisms could arise from non-living matter. Through a series of carefully designed experiments, he demonstrated that microorganisms in the air were responsible for the contamination of sterile solutions. In his famous swan-neck flask experiment, he showed that broth remained sterile when protected from airborne microorganisms, but became contaminated when exposed to air. These findings provided strong evidence against spontaneous generation and supported the germ theory of disease.

In 1857, Pasteur was appointed director of scientific studies at the École Normale Supérieure. Under his leadership, the institution became a leading centre for scientific research. He implemented rigorous standards for research and education, emphasising the importance of experimental evidence and precision. Despite facing resistance from some colleagues, Pasteur's reforms elevated the school's reputation and attracted talented students and researchers.

Pasteur's contributions to microbiology and medicine extended beyond fermentation. In the late 1860s, he began studying diseases affecting silkworms, which were devastating the silk industry in France. He identified two diseases, pébrine and flacherie, caused by parasites and bacteria, respectively. By developing methods to detect and prevent these infections, he saved the silk industry from collapse. This work demonstrated the practical applications of his germ theory and reinforced his belief in the importance of disease prevention through microbial control.

In the 1870s, Pasteur turned his attention to human and animal diseases. He investigated the causes of anthrax, a deadly disease affecting livestock and humans. Through collaboration with other scientists, he identified the bacterium Bacillus anthracis as the causative agent. Building on the work of Robert Koch, who had developed methods for isolating and identifying bacteria, Pasteur created a vaccine for anthrax. He demonstrated its efficacy through public experiments, vaccinating livestock and exposing them to the anthrax bacterium. The vaccinated animals survived, while the unvaccinated ones succumbed to the disease. This success marked a significant milestone in the development of immunology and the use of vaccines to prevent infectious diseases.

Pasteur's most famous achievement came in the development of a vaccine for rabies, a deadly viral disease transmitted through the bites of infected animals. At the time, there was no effective treatment for rabies, and it was almost always fatal. Pasteur hypothesised that the rabies virus could be attenuated, or weakened, to create a vaccine. He conducted experiments on infected animals, gradually weakening the virus by passing it through a series of rabbits. In 1885, Pasteur tested his rabies vaccine on a nine-year-old boy named Joseph Meister, who had been severely bitten by a rabid dog. The boy was given a series of injections over several days, and he recovered without developing rabies. This breakthrough not only saved Meister's life but also established the principle of using attenuated viruses for vaccination.

The success of the rabies vaccine brought Pasteur international acclaim and further solidified his legacy as a pioneer in microbiology and medicine. In 1888, the Pasteur Institute was established in Paris, dedicated to the study of infectious diseases and the development of vaccines. Pasteur served as its director, overseeing groundbreaking research and training a new generation of scientists. The institute became a leading centre for microbiological research and continues to play a crucial role in public health to this day.

Throughout his career, Pasteur faced numerous challenges and setbacks, including opposition from some members of the scientific community and personal health struggles. He suffered a severe stroke in 1868, which left him partially paralysed, but he continued to work with unwavering determination. His perseverance and commitment to scientific inquiry were driven by a deep sense of duty to improve human health and well-being.

Pasteur's contributions to science and medicine extended far beyond his own lifetime. His work laid the foundation for the fields of microbiology, immunology, and epidemiology, transforming our understanding of infectious diseases and how to prevent them. His emphasis on rigorous experimentation and empirical evidence set new standards for scientific research, and his discoveries have saved countless lives through improved food safety, disease prevention, and vaccination.

Louis Pasteur died on 28 September 1895, at the age of 72. He was buried in the Cathedral of Notre Dame in Paris, and later, his remains were moved to a crypt in the Pasteur Institute, where he rests alongside his wife, Marie. His legacy is commemorated through numerous awards, institutions, and monuments that bear his name, reflecting the profound impact of his work on science and society.

Pasteur's life and achievements serve as a testament to the power of scientific inquiry and the enduring quest to understand and improve the world around us. His discoveries have had a lasting impact on public health, agriculture, and industry, and his pioneering spirit continues to inspire scientists and researchers worldwide. Through his dedication, innovation, and perseverance, Louis Pasteur transformed the fields of microbiology and medicine, leaving an indelible mark on the history of science and human health.

George Washington

George Washington was born on 22 February 1732, in Westmoreland County, Virginia, to Augustine and Mary Ball Washington. His family was part of the Virginia gentry, which provided him with a relatively privileged upbringing. His father died when he was eleven, and his half-brother Lawrence became a significant influence, guiding his early life and providing him with opportunities to learn surveying and other skills. Washington's early education was informal, relying on tutors and the local school, where he learned the basics of reading, writing, and mathematics. He developed a talent for surveying, which became his first profession. By the age of 17, he was appointed as the official surveyor of Culpeper County, Virginia. His work as a surveyor provided him with valuable experience and a modest income, enabling him to purchase land and begin his ascent in colonial society.

In 1752, Washington's life took a significant turn when his half-brother Lawrence died, leaving him the estate of Mount Vernon. That same year, he was appointed as a district adjutant in the Virginia militia, marking the beginning of his military career. His first major assignment came in 1753 when he was sent by the Virginia Governor, Robert Dinwiddie, to deliver a message to the French, warning them to vacate the Ohio Valley, a region claimed by both France and Britain. This mission, although diplomatically unsuccessful, showcased Washington's leadership qualities and marked his entry into the complex world of colonial politics and frontier warfare.

Washington's early military career was fraught with challenges. In 1754, he led a small force to confront the French at Fort Duquesne, resulting in a skirmish that ignited the French and Indian War. During this engagement, Washington's troops suffered a defeat at Fort Necessity, but his bravery and perseverance earned him recognition. He later served as an aide to British General Edward Braddock, witnessing firsthand the disastrous defeat at the Battle of Monongahela, where Braddock was mortally wounded, and Washington's leadership in the chaotic retreat further solidified his reputation as a capable officer.

Following the French and Indian War, Washington married Martha Custis, a wealthy widow, in 1759. This marriage significantly increased his social standing and wealth, allowing him to expand Mount Vernon and delve into agricultural innovations. He focused on improving his estate, experimenting with crop rotation and other farming techniques, and became an influential figure in Virginia society. Despite his agricultural pursuits, Washington remained involved in military affairs and was increasingly drawn into the political tensions between the American colonies and Britain.

As tensions escalated into the American Revolutionary War, Washington emerged as a leading advocate for colonial resistance. In 1775, the Second Continental Congress appointed him as the Commander-in-Chief of the Continental Army. Washington faced immense challenges, including inadequate supplies, training, and funding for his troops. Despite these obstacles, he demonstrated remarkable strategic acumen, most notably in the daring surprise attack on Trenton in 1776, where his crossing of the Delaware River led to a crucial victory against the Hessian forces. This victory boosted the morale of the Continental Army and revitalised the revolutionary cause.

Washington's leadership during the harsh winter at Valley Forge in 1777-1778 exemplified his resilience and commitment. Despite severe shortages of food, clothing, and shelter, he worked tirelessly to train and reorganise his troops, instilling discipline and perseverance. His ability to maintain the cohesion and fighting spirit of the Continental Army during these difficult times was instrumental in sustaining the revolutionary effort.

Washington's strategic brilliance was further demonstrated in the Southern Campaigns, where he coordinated with General Nathanael Greene and French forces under General Rochambeau. This culminated in the decisive victory at the Siege of Yorktown in 1781, where British General Cornwallis's surrender effectively ended major combat operations and secured American independence. Throughout the war, Washington's leadership, adaptability, and ability to inspire his troops were critical to the success of the American Revolution.

Following the war, Washington faced the challenge of transitioning from military leadership to civilian life. He resigned his commission in 1783, returning to Mount Vernon with hopes of resuming his life as a planter. However, the weaknesses of the Articles of Confederation, which governed the newly independent states, soon became apparent, leading to calls for a stronger federal government. Washington's support was crucial in the convening of the Constitutional Convention in 1787, where he was unanimously elected as its president. His presence and leadership lent credibility to the proceedings, and the resulting United States Constitution established a new framework of government.

In 1789, Washington was unanimously elected as the first President of the United States, a position he accepted with a sense of duty and reluctance. His presidency set many precedents for the new nation, including the establishment of a Cabinet, the formulation of fiscal policies, and the principle of a peaceful transfer of power. Washington's leadership style was characterised by restraint, prudence, and a commitment to national unity. He navigated the young nation through its formative years, dealing with challenges such as the Whiskey Rebellion, the creation of a national bank, and maintaining neutrality in foreign conflicts, particularly between Britain and France.

Washington's commitment to national unity was also evident in his Farewell Address in 1796, where he declined a third term in office. In this address, he emphasised the importance of national unity, warned against the dangers of political factions and foreign alliances, and stressed the need for an educated and virtuous citizenry. His Farewell Address has since been regarded as a guiding document for American political principles and policies.

After retiring from the presidency, Washington returned to Mount Vernon, where he focused on managing his estate and engaging in agricultural experimentation. He continued to correspond with political leaders and remained a respected figure in national affairs. Despite his retirement, he was called upon once more in 1798, during the Quasi-War with France, to lead the country's military forces as Commander-in-Chief, though he did not see active service.

Washington's health began to decline towards the end of 1799. On 14 December of that year, he passed away at Mount Vernon from a severe throat infection, likely acute epiglottitis. His death was widely mourned across the nation, and he was eulogised as a paragon of virtue, leadership, and selfless service. His legacy as the "Father of His Country" endures, reflecting his central role in the founding and shaping of the United States.

Washington's contributions to American history are immeasurable. His leadership during the Revolutionary War ensured the success of the American struggle for independence. As the first President, he established the principles and practices of the executive branch, setting standards for future leaders. His emphasis on national unity, adherence to constitutional principles, and commitment to public service have left an indelible mark on the nation's political culture.

Throughout his life, Washington exemplified qualities of integrity, humility, and perseverance. His vision for a united and prosperous America guided his actions and decisions, influencing the course of the nation's development. His legacy is commemorated in numerous monuments, institutions, and public spaces bearing his name, including the capital city, Washington, D.C. His life and achievements continue to inspire and instruct, embodying the ideals of leadership, patriotism, and dedication to the common good.

Leonardo Fibonacci

Leonardo Fibonacci, born Leonardo Pisano, was an Italian mathematician from Pisa, likely born around 1170. His father, Guglielmo Bonacci, was a wealthy merchant who directed a trading post in Bugia, a port in the North African coast, present-day Algeria. This position exposed Fibonacci to the diverse mathematical practices of different cultures, which played a pivotal role in his later works. Fibonacci travelled extensively with his father, gaining knowledge of the Hindu-Arabic numeral system, which was vastly superior to the Roman numerals used in Europe at the time. This numeral system allowed for easier and more efficient calculations, a fact that fascinated Fibonacci.

In 1202, Fibonacci published "Liber Abaci" (The Book of Calculation), introducing the Hindu-Arabic numeral system to Europe. The book was revolutionary, advocating the use of these numerals in place of Roman numerals for arithmetic operations. Fibonacci demonstrated how the new system could simplify calculations, such as addition, subtraction, multiplication, and division. "Liber Abaci" also included various practical applications, such as conversions of currency, weight, and measures, which were particularly useful for merchants. The adoption of the Hindu-Arabic numeral system was slow but eventually led to its widespread use in Europe, profoundly impacting commerce, engineering, and science.

In "Liber Abaci," Fibonacci also presented a number sequence now known as the Fibonacci sequence. This sequence begins with 0 and 1, and each subsequent number is the sum of the two preceding ones: 0, 1, 1, 2, 3, 5, 8, 13, and so on. Although this sequence had been previously described in Indian mathematics, Fibonacci's work introduced it to the Western world. The sequence appears in various natural phenomena, such as the arrangement of leaves on a stem, the branching of trees, the flowering of artichokes, and the spiral patterns of shells. It has since become an important concept in mathematics and science, symbolising growth patterns and natural order.

Fibonacci's contributions to mathematics extended beyond the "Liber Abaci." In his "Practica Geometriae," he addressed geometric problems and methods, including the calculation of areas and volumes, and solutions to equations. This work showcased his deep understanding of geometry and his ability to apply mathematical concepts to practical problems. He also wrote "Flos" and "Liber Quadratorum," which focused on number theory and algebra. "Flos" addressed problems posed by Johannes of Palermo, including the solution to cubic equations, while "Liber Quadratorum" dealt with the properties of square numbers and the solutions to Diophantine equations, which seek integer solutions to polynomial equations.

Fibonacci's work influenced subsequent generations of mathematicians, including the Italian scholars of the Renaissance who further developed algebra and arithmetic. His introduction of the Hindu-Arabic numeral system facilitated advances in mathematics, science, and engineering, as it provided a more efficient and practical means of computation. The Fibonacci sequence has found applications in various fields, from biology and art to computer algorithms and financial markets.

Despite the profound impact of his work, much of Fibonacci's life remains shrouded in mystery. He likely spent most of his later years in Pisa, continuing his studies and writing. His contributions were recognised by the Republic of Pisa, which honoured him for his work and influence. Fibonacci's writings reflect his broad knowledge and curiosity, his ability to synthesise information from different cultures, and his skill in presenting complex concepts in an accessible manner.

Fibonacci's legacy endures not only in the mathematical concepts that bear his name but also in the broader influence of his work on European mathematics. His introduction of the Hindu-Arabic numeral system was a turning point in the history of mathematics, paving the way for the scientific and technological advancements of the Renaissance and beyond. The Fibonacci sequence continues to be a source of fascination and inspiration, illustrating the inherent patterns and structures of the natural world. His work exemplifies the power of cross-cultural exchange and the enduring impact of mathematical innovation on human knowledge and progress.

Nicolaus Copernicus

Nicolaus Copernicus was born on 19 February 1473 in Toruń, in the Kingdom of Poland. His father, Nicolaus Copernicus Sr., was a wealthy merchant, and his mother, Barbara Watzenrode, came from a prominent family. After his father's death when Copernicus was about ten years old, his uncle, Lucas Watzenrode, the bishop of Warmia, took responsibility for his upbringing and education. This influential connection ensured that Copernicus received a solid foundation in the humanities and sciences.

Copernicus began his higher education at the University of Kraków (now Jagiellonian University) in 1491. There, he studied a variety of subjects including astronomy, mathematics, philosophy, and the liberal arts. Kraków was a significant centre of learning in the Renaissance period, and Copernicus was exposed to the works of ancient Greek and Roman scholars, which influenced his later thinking. Despite not graduating, his time at Kraków played a crucial role in shaping his intellectual development.

In 1496, Copernicus travelled to Italy to continue his education. He enrolled at the University of Bologna, where he studied canon law, as well as mathematics and astronomy. During his time in Bologna, he met the renowned astronomer Domenico Maria Novara da Ferrara, who became his mentor. Under Novara's guidance, Copernicus began to question the geocentric model of the universe, which placed the Earth at the centre, a view that had dominated Western thought for over a thousand years.

After Bologna, Copernicus moved to the University of Padua, where he studied medicine. This was a practical decision, as a medical qualification would provide him with a stable career. He also continued his astronomical studies during this period. In 1503, he received a doctorate in canon law from the University of Ferrara, which allowed him to return to Poland with a comprehensive education in multiple disciplines.

Upon returning to Poland, Copernicus assumed various positions within the church, including administrative and medical roles. He served as a canon at Frombork Cathedral, where he had access to resources and the time to pursue his astronomical research. His duties included managing the cathedral's finances, overseeing local economic issues, and practicing medicine, which provided him with a stable income and the freedom to focus on his scientific interests.

Copernicus began to develop his heliocentric theory during his time at Frombork. This theory proposed that the Sun, rather than the Earth, was at the centre of the universe, and that the Earth and other planets revolved around it. This was a radical departure from the widely accepted geocentric model, which was based on the work of Ptolemy and supported by the Catholic Church. Copernicus's ideas were initially met with scepticism and caution, as they challenged the established worldview and theological doctrines.

By 1514, Copernicus had outlined his heliocentric theory in a manuscript known as the "Commentariolus" (Little Commentary). He circulated this among a small group of trusted colleagues, seeking their feedback and support. The "Commentariolus" outlined the basic principles of his theory, including the idea that the Earth rotates daily on its axis and orbits the Sun annually. These concepts were revolutionary and laid the groundwork for his later, more comprehensive work.

Copernicus continued to refine his ideas over the next few decades, conducting detailed observations and mathematical calculations. He sought to address the complexities of planetary motion that the geocentric model could not adequately explain. His observations of planetary positions and movements supported his heliocentric model, providing a more coherent and simpler explanation for celestial phenomena.

In 1532, Copernicus completed the manuscript of his magnum opus, "De revolutionibus orbium coelestium" (On the Revolutions of the Heavenly Spheres). However, he hesitated to publish it, aware of the potential controversy and backlash from the religious and academic communities. He continued to revise and refine the work, ensuring that his arguments were as robust and persuasive as possible.

In 1543, at the urging of his close friends and colleagues, including the mathematician Georg Joachim Rheticus, Copernicus finally agreed to publish "De revolutionibus." Rheticus, who had studied with Copernicus and was a strong advocate of his ideas, played a crucial role in persuading him to share his groundbreaking work with the world. The book was published just before Copernicus's death, and a copy was reportedly placed in his hands on his deathbed.

"De revolutionibus" outlined Copernicus's heliocentric theory in detail, presenting mathematical models and observations that supported his revolutionary ideas. The book challenged the established geocentric model and proposed a new framework for understanding the cosmos. It consisted of six books, covering various aspects of astronomy, including the movements of celestial bodies, the structure of the universe, and the mathematics underlying his theory.

The publication of "De revolutionibus" marked a turning point in the history of astronomy and science. Although it was initially met with resistance and controversy, Copernicus's heliocentric model gradually gained acceptance among scholars. His work laid the foundation for the Scientific Revolution, influencing later astronomers such as Johannes Kepler and Galileo Galilei. Kepler refined Copernicus's ideas by introducing elliptical orbits, while Galileo's observations with the telescope provided further evidence for the heliocentric model.

Copernicus's heliocentric theory had profound implications for the way humanity understood its place in the universe. It challenged the anthropocentric view that placed humans at the centre of creation and opened the door to a more expansive and dynamic understanding of the cosmos. His work also exemplified the power of careful observation, mathematical rigor, and the willingness to question established doctrines in the pursuit of knowledge.

In addition to his contributions to astronomy, Copernicus made significant advances in economics and mathematics. He developed the quantity theory of money, which explained the relationship between money supply and price levels. This theory was an early contribution to the field of economics, demonstrating his intellectual versatility and wide-ranging interests.

Copernicus's life was characterised by a dedication to knowledge and a commitment to challenging established ideas through careful observation and analysis. His heliocentric theory, although initially controversial, ultimately transformed our understanding of the universe and laid the groundwork for modern astronomy. His work exemplifies the spirit of scientific inquiry and the transformative power of innovative thinking. Nicolaus Copernicus's legacy endures as a testament to the profound impact of questioning conventional wisdom and seeking deeper truths about the natural world. His contributions continue to inspire scientists and thinkers, reminding us of the importance of curiosity, perseverance, and intellectual courage in the pursuit of knowledge.

Johannes Kepler

Johannes Kepler was born on 27 December 1571 in Weil der Stadt, a small town in the Holy Roman Empire, now in Germany. His family was modest and his father, Heinrich Kepler, was a mercenary who abandoned the family when Johannes was young. His mother, Katharina Guldenmann, was an herbalist and healer. Kepler's early education was influenced by his mother's interest in the natural world and his grandfather's encouragement. He showed an early talent for mathematics and astronomy, despite struggling with poor health and a vision impairment.

Kepler's path to higher education began at the Protestant seminary in Maulbronn. He excelled academically and earned a scholarship to study at the University of Tübingen. There, he studied under the mathematician Michael Maestlin, who introduced him to the Copernican heliocentric system, which posited that the Earth and other planets revolve around the Sun. This idea profoundly influenced Kepler, despite the prevailing Ptolemaic geocentric model.

Kepler intended to become a Lutheran minister but was instead offered a position teaching mathematics and astronomy at the Protestant school in Graz, Austria, in 1594. His role included producing annual astrological calendars, which, while scientifically dubious, were popular and respected at the time. In Graz, Kepler began his astronomical investigations and published his first significant work, "Mysterium Cosmographicum" (The Cosmographic Mystery) in 1596. In this work, Kepler defended the Copernican system and proposed that the orbits of the planets could be explained by nested Platonic solids, linking geometry with cosmology in a novel way.

In 1600, Kepler met the Danish astronomer Tycho Brahe, who was then the imperial mathematician for Emperor Rudolf II in Prague. Tycho invited Kepler to join his team of astronomers. Kepler accepted the position in 1601 and moved to Prague. Tycho's death later that year left Kepler with access to

Tycho's extensive and precise observational data, which became crucial for Kepler's later work.

Kepler's analysis of Tycho's data led to the formulation of his three laws of planetary motion, which revolutionised the understanding of celestial mechanics. The first law, stated in 1609 in his book "Astronomia Nova" (New Astronomy), posited that planets move in elliptical orbits with the Sun at one focus, rather than in perfect circles as previously believed. This law challenged the long-held Aristotelian and Ptolemaic views of celestial perfection.

The second law, also presented in "Astronomia Nova," stated that a line segment joining a planet and the Sun sweeps out equal areas during equal intervals of time. This meant that planets move faster when they are closer to the Sun and slower when they are farther away, describing the variable speeds of planets in their orbits.

Kepler's third law, formulated in 1619 and published in "Harmonices Mundi" (Harmony of the Worlds), established that the square of a planet's orbital period is proportional to the cube of the semi-major axis of its orbit. This law provided a precise mathematical relationship between the distances of the planets from the Sun and their orbital periods, further substantiating the heliocentric model and demonstrating the harmony and order of the cosmos.

These laws not only supported the Copernican system but also laid the groundwork for Isaac Newton's theory of universal gravitation. Kepler's meticulous work showed that the motions of the planets could be described by simple mathematical principles, fundamentally altering the scientific view of the universe.

In addition to his work on planetary motion, Kepler made significant contributions to optics. His book "Astronomiae Pars Optica" (The Optical Part of Astronomy), published in 1604, was a groundbreaking study of the nature of light and vision. Kepler explained how the human eye works, described the principles of pinhole cameras, and discussed the inverse square law of light intensity. His work on optics also led to improvements in telescopic design, influencing the development of the Keplerian telescope, which used two convex lenses to provide a wider field of view and greater magnification than Galileo's design.

Kepler's personal life was fraught with difficulties. His Protestant faith subjected him to persecution during the Counter-Reformation. In 1600, he was forced to leave Graz due to religious conflicts and later had to flee from Linz during the Thirty Years' War. Kepler also faced financial struggles and personal tragedies, including the death of several of his children and his first wife, Barbara Müller.

Despite these challenges, Kepler remained dedicated to his scientific work. He served as the imperial mathematician to three Holy Roman Emperors: Rudolf II, Matthias, and Ferdinand II. His duties included astrological and astronomical tasks, such as creating calendars and horoscopes, but he continued his research and writing.

In 1627, Kepler published the "Rudolphine Tables," named in honour of Emperor Rudolf II. These astronomical tables were based on Tycho Brahe's observations and Kepler's laws of planetary motion. They provided the most accurate astronomical data of the time and were used by astronomers and navigators for many years. The "Rudolphine Tables" marked a significant advancement in celestial mapping and prediction.

Kepler also delved into the field of astrology, although his approach was more scientific and critical than that of his contemporaries. While he recognised astrology's historical and cultural significance, he sought to separate its empirical aspects from superstition. His pragmatic and rational perspective on astrology reflected his broader commitment to scientific inquiry and scepticism of unfounded beliefs.

In the final years of his life, Kepler faced increasing hardship. He was unable to secure a stable position, and his financial situation deteriorated. He spent his last years moving between cities, seeking support for his work. Kepler died on 15 November 1630 in Regensburg, Germany, while attempting to collect an overdue salary from the Imperial Treasury. He was buried in an unmarked grave, his burial place lost to history due to the turmoil of the Thirty Years' War.

Kepler's legacy is profound and far-reaching. His laws of planetary motion provided the foundation for modern celestial mechanics and were crucial to the later work of Newton, who acknowledged Kepler's contributions in his own development of the law of universal gravitation. Kepler's work demonstrated the power of mathematical principles in describing the natural world, bridging the gap between Renaissance humanism and the scientific revolution.

Kepler's contributions to optics and his development of the Keplerian telescope significantly advanced the field of observational astronomy. His understanding of the behaviour of light and vision influenced subsequent scientific research and technological innovation in optics. The Keplerian telescope design is still in use today, a testament to the enduring impact of his work.

Kepler's perseverance in the face of personal and professional adversity exemplifies his dedication to scientific discovery. His ability to navigate the political and religious complexities of his time, while pursuing groundbreaking research, highlights his intellectual resilience and commitment to knowledge.

Kepler's integration of mathematical rigor with empirical observation set new standards for scientific methodology. His emphasis on precise measurement and the use of mathematical relationships to describe natural phenomena helped establish the principles of modern science. Kepler's holistic approach, combining astronomy, mathematics, and natural philosophy, reflects the interdisciplinary nature of his thinking and his influence on various scientific fields.

The recognition of Kepler's achievements has grown over time. He is celebrated as one of the key figures in the history of science, and his work continues to inspire astronomers, mathematicians, and scientists across disciplines. Monuments, institutions, and awards bearing his name honour his contributions and legacy.

Kepler's life and work remind us of the importance of curiosity, perseverance, and the willingness to challenge established beliefs in the pursuit of truth. His discoveries not only transformed our understanding of the universe but also laid the groundwork for the scientific advancements that followed. Johannes Kepler's enduring legacy is a testament to the power of human inquiry and the quest for knowledge that transcends the challenges and limitations of any era.

Michael Faraday

Michael Faraday was born on 22 September 1791 in Newington Butts, a suburb of London, into a humble family. His father, James Faraday, was a blacksmith, and his mother, Margaret Hastwell, came from a farming background. Despite their limited means, the family valued education and instilled a sense of curiosity in young Michael. Faraday received a basic education and began working at the age of 14 as an apprentice to George Riebau, a local bookbinder and bookseller. This job provided him with access to a wealth of books and knowledge, which he eagerly absorbed.

During his apprenticeship, Faraday developed a keen interest in science, particularly in electricity and chemistry. He read extensively, including Isaac Watts's "The Improvement of the Mind" and Jane Marcet's "Conversations on Chemistry," which inspired his early experiments. Faraday's enthusiasm and self-taught knowledge caught the attention of his employer, who encouraged his scientific pursuits.

In 1812, Faraday attended a series of lectures by the eminent chemist Humphry Davy at the Royal Institution. Fascinated by Davy's work, Faraday took meticulous notes and bound them into a book, which he sent to Davy along with a letter expressing his admiration and desire to work in science. Davy was impressed and offered Faraday a position as his assistant in 1813. This opportunity was a turning point in Faraday's life, providing him with hands-on experience in a professional laboratory setting.

As Davy's assistant, Faraday accompanied him on a European tour, where he met and interacted with leading scientists of the time. This exposure broadened Faraday's scientific horizons and allowed him to build valuable connections. Upon returning to England, Faraday continued to work at the Royal Institution, initially focusing on chemistry. He conducted numerous experiments, leading to significant discoveries, including the liquefaction of chlorine and the identification of new compounds such as benzene.

Faraday's work in chemistry earned him recognition and respect within the scientific community. In 1820, he was appointed as the Superintendent of the House at the Royal Institution, and in 1825, he became the Director of the Laboratory. These positions allowed him to pursue his research with greater independence and authority. Faraday's contributions to chemistry were substantial, but his most groundbreaking work was in the field of electromagnetism.

In 1821, building on the work of Hans Christian Ørsted and André-Marie Ampère, Faraday discovered the phenomenon of electromagnetic rotation. He demonstrated that a magnetic field could induce a circular motion in a wire carrying an electric current, effectively creating the first electric motor. This experiment laid the foundation for the development of electromechanical devices and marked the beginning of Faraday's lifelong investigation into electromagnetism.

Faraday's most significant discovery came in 1831 with the demonstration of electromagnetic induction. He showed that a changing magnetic field could induce an electric current in a conductor. Faraday's experiments involved moving a magnet through a coil of wire, which generated an electric current in the wire. This discovery was crucial, as it provided the basic principles for the generation of electricity by mechanical means, leading to the development of electric generators and transformers.

Faraday's work on electromagnetic induction was published in his "Experimental Researches in Electricity," a series of papers that detailed his experiments and findings. His clear and methodical approach to experimentation and his emphasis on empirical evidence set new standards for scientific research. Faraday's discoveries not only advanced the field of electromagnetism but also had practical applications that transformed industry and technology.

In addition to his work on electromagnetism, Faraday made significant contributions to the field of electrochemistry. He formulated the laws of electrolysis, which describe the relationship between the amount of electric charge passed through an electrolyte and the amount of substance deposited at the electrodes. Faraday's laws of electrolysis provided a quantitative understanding of the processes involved in electrochemical reactions and laid the groundwork for the development of electroplating and other industrial applications.

Faraday's contributions to science extended beyond his experimental work. He was an exceptional communicator and educator, dedicated to making science accessible to the public. He delivered numerous lectures at the Royal Institution, including the famous Christmas Lectures for young audiences. His ability to explain complex scientific concepts in a clear and engaging manner inspired generations of scientists and contributed to the popularisation of science.

Despite his lack of formal education and social disadvantages, Faraday achieved remarkable success through his intellect, curiosity, and perseverance. He was elected a Fellow of the Royal Society in 1824 and received numerous honours and awards throughout his career, including the Royal Medal, the Copley Medal, and the Rumford Medal. Faraday's humility and modesty were notable; he declined offers of knighthood and the presidency of the Royal Society, preferring to remain focused on his scientific work.

Faraday's contributions to science were not limited to his own discoveries. He mentored and collaborated with other scientists, fostering a spirit of cooperation and shared inquiry. His work had a profound influence on subsequent developments in physics and chemistry, and his principles of electromagnetic induction remain fundamental to modern electrical engineering.

In the latter part of his career, Faraday continued to conduct research and deliver lectures, although his health began to decline. He suffered from memory loss and other health issues, which gradually limited his ability to work. Despite these challenges, Faraday remained dedicated to science and maintained his curiosity and passion for discovery.

Michael Faraday died on 25 August 1867 at his home in Hampton Court, Surrey. His legacy is commemorated in numerous ways, including the naming of the unit of capacitance, the farad, in his honour. Faraday's contributions to science and technology have left an enduring impact, shaping the modern world and inspiring future generations of scientists.

Faraday's life and achievements exemplify the power of curiosity, determination, and intellectual rigor. His groundbreaking discoveries in electromagnetism and electrochemistry laid the foundation for many of the technological advancements that define contemporary society. Faraday's commitment to public education and his ability to communicate complex ideas to a broad audience contributed to the spread of scientific knowledge and the popularisation of science.

Faraday's work demonstrated the importance of empirical evidence and experimentation in scientific inquiry. His meticulous approach to research, combined with his creativity and insight, enabled him to make significant contributions to multiple fields of science. Faraday's legacy serves as a testament to the transformative power of scientific discovery and the enduring impact of individual contributions to the advancement of human knowledge.

Michael Faraday's life story is one of triumph over adversity, driven by a relentless pursuit of understanding and a passion for discovery. His achievements continue to inspire and inform the scientific community, highlighting the importance of curiosity, perseverance, and the quest for knowledge. Faraday's contributions have had a lasting influence on the fields of physics and chemistry, and his legacy remains a cornerstone of modern science and technology.

James Watt

James Watt was born on 19 January 1736 in Greenock, Scotland, a thriving port town. His father, James Watt Sr., was a shipwright and merchant, and his mother, Agnes Muirhead, came from a distinguished family. Watt was a frail child, suffering from frequent illnesses, which often kept him away from school. However, he was a keen observer and a quick learner, spending much of his time at home reading and experimenting with his father's tools. Watt's early education was informal, but his inquisitive nature and his family's supportive environment nurtured his developing interest in science and engineering.

Watt's formal education began in Greenock, where he attended local schools. Although his attendance was sporadic due to his health, his teachers recognised his aptitude for mathematics and mechanics. At the age of 17, Watt moved to Glasgow to learn the trade of instrument making. He became an apprentice to a local instrument maker, but his tenure was cut short after just a year due to the limited opportunities in Glasgow. Determined to further his skills, Watt moved to London in 1755 to apprentice with John Morgan, a renowned instrument maker. His time in London was challenging, as he worked long hours under demanding conditions, but he honed his craft and became proficient in making precision instruments.

In 1757, Watt returned to Glasgow and set up his own workshop at the University of Glasgow. He was appointed as the university's mathematical instrument maker, a position that allowed him to repair and create scientific instruments for the faculty. It was here that Watt began his lifelong association with academia and industry. The university provided him with access to a network of influential scholars, including Professor John Robison and economist Adam Smith. These connections enriched his knowledge and broadened his horizons.

Watt's first significant breakthrough came in 1764 when he was asked to repair a model of a Newcomen steam engine. The Newcomen engine, invented in 1712, was used primarily for pumping water out of mines but was notoriously inefficient. Watt recognised that the engine's inefficiency was due to the significant loss of steam and heat. Through a series of experiments, Watt devised a separate condenser, which dramatically improved the engine's efficiency. This innovation allowed the steam to be condensed in a separate chamber, maintaining the temperature of the cylinder and reducing fuel consumption.

In 1769, Watt received a patent for his separate condenser, marking the beginning of his career as an inventor and engineer. However, he lacked the financial resources to develop his ideas further. In 1775, he partnered with Matthew Boulton, a wealthy industrialist with a factory in Birmingham. Boulton provided the financial backing and business acumen that Watt needed to bring his inventions to market. The partnership between Watt and Boulton proved to be highly successful, combining Watt's technical genius with Boulton's entrepreneurial skills.

Together, they established Boulton & Watt, which became a leading engineering firm. Watt continued to improve his steam engine, developing additional features such as the rotary motion, the double-acting engine, and the parallel motion linkage. The rotary motion allowed the engine to drive machinery, such as mills and factories, expanding its applications beyond pumping water. The double-acting engine increased efficiency by using steam on both sides of the piston, while the parallel motion linkage enabled the engine to produce smooth, consistent motion.

Watt's innovations transformed the steam engine into a versatile and powerful tool, driving the Industrial Revolution. Factories, mills, and mines across Britain and beyond adopted Watt's engines, revolutionising manufacturing processes and increasing productivity. The widespread use of steam power spurred economic growth, urbanisation, and technological advancements, reshaping society and industry.

Watt was also an inventor of several other devices and improvements. He invented the flyball governor, a device used to regulate the speed of steam engines automatically. This invention ensured the safe and efficient operation of machinery, further enhancing the utility of steam power. Watt also developed a copying machine, which allowed for the reproduction of documents, contributing to administrative efficiency in businesses and government offices.

Despite his numerous achievements, Watt was a humble and private individual. He was more interested in practical solutions and incremental improvements than in theoretical work. His approach to engineering was methodical and empirical, relying on experimentation and observation to solve problems. Watt's contributions to engineering were not limited to his own inventions; he also mentored and collaborated with other engineers and scientists, fostering a spirit of innovation and cooperation.

Watt's personal life was marked by both triumphs and tragedies. He married his cousin, Margaret Miller, in 1764, and they had five children, though only two survived to adulthood. Margaret died in 1773, and Watt remarried Ann MacGregor in 1776, with whom he had two more children. Watt faced health issues throughout his life, including debilitating headaches and depression, but he remained dedicated to his work and continued to innovate until his retirement.

In 1800, Watt retired from active involvement in the business, leaving the company in the capable hands of his sons, James Watt Jr. and Gregory Watt, and his partner, Matthew Boulton. He spent his later years in relative quiet, focusing on refining his inventions and enjoying his estate in Handsworth, near Birmingham. Watt continued to receive honours and recognition for his contributions to engineering and science, including election to the Royal Society and the French Academy of Sciences.

Watt's impact on the world extended far beyond his lifetime. His innovations in steam engine technology laid the foundation for modern mechanical engineering and powered the Industrial Revolution. The principles of steam power that Watt developed were applied to transportation, including steamboats and locomotives, transforming travel and commerce. Watt's work also influenced the development of thermodynamics and the study of energy, shaping the future of engineering and science.

James Watt died on 25 August 1819 at the age of 83. He was buried in St. Mary's Church, Handsworth, alongside his business partner, Matthew Boulton. Watt's legacy is commemorated in various ways, including the unit of power, the watt, named in his honour. Monuments, buildings, and institutions bearing his name celebrate his contributions to engineering and his role in the Industrial Revolution.

Watt's life and achievements exemplify the power of innovation, perseverance, and practical problem-solving. His ability to improve existing technologies and develop new solutions transformed industries and laid the groundwork for future advancements. Watt's work ethic, intellectual curiosity, and dedication to improving society through engineering have left an enduring mark on history.

James Watt's contributions to engineering and industry continue to be celebrated and studied. His inventions and improvements to the steam engine were pivotal in the transition to a mechanised and industrialised world. Watt's work demonstrated the importance of collaboration between inventors and entrepreneurs, highlighting the value of combining technical expertise with business acumen. His legacy serves as an inspiration to engineers and innovators, reminding us of the profound impact that practical, well-executed ideas can have on the world.

Through his ingenuity and determination, James Watt changed the course of history, enabling the widespread use of steam power and driving the Industrial Revolution. His life and work exemplify the transformative power of engineering and innovation, illustrating how one individual's contributions can reshape industries, economies, and societies. Watt's achievements continue to influence modern engineering, and his legacy endures as a testament to the enduring impact of scientific and technological progress.

Alexander Fleming

Alexander Fleming was born on 6 August 1881 in Lochfield, a farm near Darvel in Ayrshire, Scotland. He was the seventh of eight children born to Hugh Fleming, a farmer, and his second wife, Grace Stirling Morton. Growing up in a rural environment, Fleming developed a strong sense of curiosity and a keen interest in the natural world. His early education was at the local Loudoun Moor School and later at Darvel School. After his father died when Fleming was seven, his mother continued to run the family farm with the help of her older children. In 1895, Fleming moved to London to live with his elder brother, Tom, who was a practicing physician. Fleming attended the Regent Street Polytechnic, where he studied business and commerce, but his interest in the sciences soon led him to pursue a medical career.

In 1901, Fleming enrolled at St Mary's Hospital Medical School in Paddington, London, thanks to a scholarship. He excelled in his studies and graduated with distinction in 1906. At St Mary's, Fleming joined the research department of Sir Almroth Wright, a pioneer in immunology and vaccine therapy. Under Wright's mentorship, Fleming developed a strong foundation in bacteriology and experimental methods. Wright's influence was significant, shaping Fleming's scientific approach and encouraging his interest in research.

During World War I, Fleming served as a captain in the Royal Army Medical Corps, working in battlefield hospitals in France. His experiences treating wounded soldiers exposed him to the severe limitations of existing antiseptics, which often caused more harm than good by destroying both healthy and infected tissues. These observations reinforced his determination to find more effective methods of combating infections.

After the war, Fleming returned to St Mary's Hospital and resumed his research. In 1921, he discovered lysozyme, an enzyme with mild antiseptic properties found in bodily fluids such as tears, saliva, and mucus. While this discovery did not lead to an immediate breakthrough in infection control, it demonstrated the potential of naturally occurring substances to combat bacteria without harming human tissues. Fleming's work on lysozyme laid the groundwork for his later discoveries.

In 1928, while conducting experiments on influenza, Fleming made a serendipitous observation that would revolutionise medicine. Upon returning from a holiday, he noticed that a petri dish containing Staphylococcus bacteria had been accidentally contaminated by a mould, later identified as Penicillium notatum. The area around the mould was clear of bacteria, indicating that the mould was producing a substance that inhibited bacterial growth. Fleming named this substance penicillin.

Fleming recognised the potential of penicillin as an antibacterial agent, capable of killing a wide range of harmful bacteria while being non-toxic to humans. He conducted further experiments to confirm its effectiveness and published his findings in 1929. Despite the significance of his discovery, Fleming faced challenges in isolating and producing penicillin in large quantities. The instability and difficulty of purifying the compound hindered its immediate development and application.

For several years, Fleming's work on penicillin received little attention. However, in the early 1940s, a team of scientists at the University of Oxford, including Howard Florey and Ernst Boris Chain, revisited Fleming's research. With advancements in chemical techniques and the urgency of World War II driving the need for effective antibiotics, they succeeded in mass-producing penicillin. Their efforts led to the widespread use of penicillin in treating bacterial infections, saving countless lives during and after the war.

Penicillin's success marked the beginning of the antibiotic era, transforming medical practice and revolutionising the treatment of bacterial infections. Fleming's initial discovery was crucial, but it was the collaborative efforts of scientists and pharmaceutical companies that enabled penicillin's mass production and global distribution. The impact of penicillin was profound, reducing the mortality rates from infections such as pneumonia, tuberculosis, and syphilis, and allowing for safer surgical procedures.

Fleming's contributions to medicine were widely recognised. In 1945, he, along with Florey and Chain, was awarded the Nobel Prize in Physiology or Medicine for the discovery and development of penicillin. This accolade cemented Fleming's place in medical history and highlighted the importance of his work in improving public health. Despite his fame, Fleming remained modest about his achievements, often attributing the success of penicillin to chance and the collaborative efforts of his colleagues.

In addition to his work on penicillin, Fleming continued to research bacteriology and immunology throughout his career. He made significant contributions to the understanding of bacterial resistance and the role of antiseptics in wound treatment. His scientific approach was characterised by meticulous observation, a willingness to embrace unexpected results, and a commitment to improving patient care.

Fleming's personal life was marked by his dedication to his work. He married Sarah Marion McElroy in 1915, and they had one son, Robert, who followed in his father's footsteps to become a general practitioner. Sarah's support was instrumental in Fleming's career, providing stability and encouragement throughout his scientific endeavours. After Sarah's death in 1949, Fleming married Dr Amalia Koutsouri-Vourekas, a Greek colleague, in 1953.

Fleming was a member of several prestigious scientific organisations, including the Royal Society, and received numerous honours and awards throughout his lifetime. He was knighted in 1944, becoming Sir Alexander Fleming in recognition of his contributions to medicine and science. Despite his accolades, Fleming remained dedicated to his research and continued to work at St Mary's Hospital until his death.

Alexander Fleming died on 11 March 1955 of a heart attack at his home in London. He was buried in St Paul's Cathedral, a testament to his significant impact on medicine and his enduring legacy. Fleming's life and work have left an indelible mark on the field of bacteriology and the treatment of infectious diseases.

Fleming's discovery of penicillin not only revolutionised medicine but also paved the way for the development of other antibiotics, transforming healthcare and saving millions of lives. His work demonstrated the importance of scientific curiosity, rigorous experimentation, and the willingness to explore unconventional paths. Fleming's legacy continues to inspire researchers and healthcare professionals in the ongoing fight against bacterial infections and antibiotic resistance.

The development and mass production of penicillin also highlighted the importance of interdisciplinary collaboration and the role of government and industry in advancing scientific discoveries. The success of penicillin underscored the need for continued investment in research and development to address emerging health challenges.

Fleming's contributions to science and medicine are commemorated in various ways, including institutions, awards, and monuments bearing his name. His work serves as a reminder of the profound impact that individual discoveries can have on society and the importance of perseverance and collaboration in scientific advancement.

Alexander Fleming's life story is one of serendipity, dedication, and transformative impact. His discovery of penicillin, coupled with the efforts of his colleagues and subsequent advancements in antibiotic production, revolutionised the treatment of bacterial infections and ushered in a new era of medical science. Fleming's legacy endures as a testament to the power of scientific inquiry and the profound ways in which it can improve human health and well-being.

Gregor Mendel

Gregor Mendel was born on 20 July 1822 in Heinzendorf, a small village in the Austrian Empire, now part of the Czech Republic. He was the son of Anton and Rosine Mendel, farmers with limited means but a deep appreciation for education. Mendel showed early academic promise, attending a local school where his abilities in science and mathematics became evident. Despite the financial constraints of his family, Mendel's academic talents led him to pursue further education, thanks to the support of his parents and local benefactors.

In 1843, Mendel entered the Augustinian Abbey of St Thomas in Brno (then Brünn), a decision influenced by both his intellectual pursuits and his financial situation. Joining the monastery provided Mendel with the stability and resources to continue his education. He took the religious name Gregor and was ordained as a priest in 1847. The abbey was a centre of learning, and Mendel's superiors recognised his potential, encouraging him to further his studies in science.

In 1851, Mendel was sent to the University of Vienna, where he studied under the guidance of prominent scientists such as Christian Doppler and Franz Unger. His education at Vienna focused on physics, mathematics, and natural sciences, providing him with a solid foundation in scientific methodology and experimental design. This period of study was crucial in shaping Mendel's analytical skills and his understanding of biological processes.

Upon returning to the abbey in 1853, Mendel was appointed as a teacher at a local secondary school, where he taught physics and natural history. In addition to his teaching duties, Mendel began conducting experiments in the abbey's garden, focusing on plant hybridisation. His choice of research subject was influenced by previous work on plant breeding and the need to understand the mechanisms of inheritance.

Mendel's experiments, conducted between 1856 and 1863, involved the cultivation and cross-breeding of pea plants (Pisum sativum). He selected pea plants because they had easily observable traits, such as flower colour, seed shape, and pod appearance, and they could be easily manipulated for controlled breeding experiments. Mendel meticulously tracked the inheritance of these traits over multiple generations, recording his observations with precision and care.

Through his experiments, Mendel formulated several key principles of inheritance. He discovered that traits are passed from parents to offspring in discrete units, which he called "factors" (now known as genes). Mendel observed that these factors segregate independently during the formation of reproductive cells, and that some traits are dominant while others are recessive. His work led to the formulation of the laws of segregation and independent assortment, which describe the patterns of inheritance for different traits.

Mendel presented his findings in 1865 at two meetings of the Natural History Society of Brno. His paper, "Experiments on Plant Hybridisation," was published in the society's journal in 1866. Despite the significance of his discoveries, Mendel's work received little attention from the scientific community during his lifetime. His ideas were ahead of their time, and the mechanisms of inheritance he described were not widely understood or appreciated by his contemporaries.

Undeterred by the lack of immediate recognition, Mendel continued his scientific pursuits, although his administrative duties as the abbot of the monastery, a position he assumed in 1868, limited his time for research. As abbot, Mendel was responsible for managing the abbey's finances and overseeing its operations, which included maintaining its agricultural lands and supporting its educational activities.

In addition to his work on genetics, Mendel conducted experiments on meteorology and beekeeping. He maintained a lifelong interest in the weather, recording detailed observations and contributing to the field of meteorology. His studies on bees, although less well-known, demonstrated his broad scientific curiosity and his commitment to understanding natural phenomena.

Mendel's personal life was characterised by his dedication to his faith, his community, and his scientific work. He was known for his humility, kindness, and intellectual rigor. Despite the challenges he faced, including health problems later in life, Mendel remained committed to his research and his responsibilities as abbot.

Mendel died on 6 January 1884 at the age of 61, largely unrecognised for his groundbreaking work in genetics. It was not until the early 20th century, more than three decades after his death, that his contributions were rediscovered and appreciated by the scientific community. In 1900, three botanists—Hugo de Vries, Carl Correns, and Erich von Tschermak—independently confirmed Mendel's findings, leading to the widespread recognition of his work and the foundation of modern genetics.

Mendel's principles of inheritance provided the framework for understanding how traits are passed from one generation to the next. His work laid the groundwork for the discovery of genes and the development of the field of genetics. The principles of dominance, segregation, and independent assortment that Mendel described are fundamental to the study of heredity and have been validated through extensive research in various organisms.

The impact of Mendel's work extends far beyond the field of genetics. His methods of controlled experimentation and statistical analysis influenced the scientific approach in biology and other disciplines. Mendel's emphasis on quantitative data and careful observation set new standards for scientific research and experimentation.

Mendel's legacy is celebrated in numerous ways. The Mendel Museum in Brno, located at the site of the Augustinian Abbey, honours his contributions to science and education. His name is associated with various scientific awards, institutions, and research centres dedicated to the study of genetics and biology. Mendel's work continues to inspire researchers and educators, highlighting the importance of curiosity, perseverance, and rigorous scientific inquiry.

Mendel's discoveries have had profound implications for agriculture, medicine, and biotechnology. Understanding the principles of inheritance has enabled the development of new crop varieties, the improvement of livestock breeds, and the advancement of personalised medicine. Mendel's work has also paved the way for the study of genetic disorders, the development of gene therapy, and the exploration of the genetic basis of complex traits.

In recent years, advances in molecular biology and genomics have built upon Mendel's foundational principles, leading to new insights into the mechanisms of inheritance and the regulation of gene expression. The discovery of DNA as the genetic material and the elucidation of its structure and function have expanded our understanding of heredity and provided new tools for genetic research and biotechnology.

Mendel's life and achievements exemplify the power of scientific inquiry and the importance of challenging established ideas through careful observation and experimentation. His work serves as a reminder of the value of curiosity, perseverance, and intellectual rigor in the pursuit of knowledge. Mendel's contributions to science have left an enduring legacy, shaping the field of genetics and transforming our understanding of the natural world.

Gregor Mendel's journey from a small village in the Austrian Empire to becoming the father of modern genetics is a testament to his dedication, intellect, and passion for science. His discoveries have had a lasting impact on biology, agriculture, medicine, and beyond, influencing the course of scientific research and the development of new technologies. Mendel's legacy continues to inspire scientists and researchers, reminding us of the profound impact that careful observation, methodical experimentation, and a relentless pursuit of knowledge can have on our understanding of the world.

Wright Brothers

Wilbur Wright was born on 16 April 1867, near Millville, Indiana, and Orville Wright was born on 19 August 1871, in Dayton, Ohio. They were two of seven children born to Milton Wright, a bishop in the Church of the United Brethren in Christ, and Susan Koerner Wright. Their father's position meant the family moved frequently, fostering a close-knit relationship among the siblings. Their mother, Susan, had a mechanical aptitude and encouraged her children's curiosity and inventiveness.

From a young age, the Wright brothers were fascinated by mechanics and flight. Their interest in aviation was sparked in 1878 when their father brought home a toy helicopter powered by rubber bands. This simple toy ignited their imagination and set them on a path that would change the world. The brothers had complementary skills and a shared passion for understanding how things worked. Wilbur was methodical and disciplined, while Orville was more adventurous and intuitive.

After finishing high school, the brothers started a printing business in 1889. They designed and built their own printing press, which they used to print newspapers, flyers, and other materials. This venture honed their skills in mechanics and business. In 1892, they shifted focus and opened a bicycle sales and repair shop called the Wright Cycle Company. The bicycle business provided them with the financial stability and technical expertise needed for their future aviation experiments. They designed and built their own bicycles, gaining valuable experience in designing and constructing precision machines.

The brothers' serious interest in flight began in 1896, when they read about the work of Otto Lilienthal, a German aviation pioneer who died in a glider crash. Inspired by Lilienthal's gliding experiments, the Wrights began to study aerodynamics and the principles of flight. They meticulously gathered information and conducted their own experiments to understand the forces involved in flight. The brothers corresponded with Octave Chanute, an aviation enthusiast and engineer, who became a mentor and provided them with valuable insights and encouragement.

In 1899, the Wright brothers began building and testing their own gliders. They focused on solving the problem of control, which they believed was the key to successful flight. They developed a three-axis control system, which allowed the pilot to steer the aircraft and maintain its equilibrium. This system, which included wing-warping for roll control, a movable rudder for yaw control, and an elevator for pitch control, was a breakthrough in aviation technology. They tested their gliders extensively at Kitty Hawk, North Carolina, chosen for its steady winds and soft sand dunes.

After several years of experimentation and incremental improvements, the Wright brothers made their first successful powered flight on 17 December 1903. The aircraft, named the Wright Flyer, was a biplane with a wingspan of 12.3 metres and powered by a 12-horsepower engine designed and built by the brothers. On that historic day, Orville piloted the first flight, which lasted 12 seconds and covered 36.5 metres. Wilbur and Orville alternated piloting the aircraft for four flights, the longest of which was piloted by Wilbur and lasted 59 seconds, covering 259.7 metres.

The Wright brothers' achievement was not just the result of building a working aircraft; it was the culmination of years of rigorous experimentation, innovation, and problem-solving. They developed a wind tunnel to test different wing shapes and gathered extensive data on lift and drag. Their methodical approach and commitment to understanding the principles of flight set them apart from other aviation pioneers of their time.

Following their success at Kitty Hawk, the Wright brothers continued to refine their designs and conduct further tests. In 1904 and 1905, they built and flew the Wright Flyer II and the Wright Flyer III, making significant improvements in control, power, and stability. By 1905, they had developed an aircraft capable of sustained, controlled flight. The Wright Flyer III was the world's first practical airplane, capable of flying for over 30 minutes and making controlled turns and circles.

Despite their achievements, the Wright brothers faced challenges in gaining recognition and financial support. They were cautious about revealing too much about their invention for fear of losing control over their patents. In 1906, they received a patent for their flying machine, covering their three-axis control system. However, scepticism from the public and scientific community persisted, and they struggled to find buyers for their aircraft.

The breakthrough came in 1908 when the Wright brothers demonstrated their aircraft to the public and the military in both the United States and Europe. Wilbur travelled to France, where he made a series of impressive flights, capturing the attention of the European aviation community and the general public. His flights in France, particularly at Le Mans and Pau, were widely covered by the press and demonstrated the capabilities of the Wright aircraft. Orville conducted similar demonstrations in the United States, including flights for the U.S. Army at Fort Myer, Virginia. During one of these demonstrations, Orville had a crash that resulted in the death of his passenger, Lieutenant Thomas Selfridge, and serious injuries to himself. Despite this tragedy, the demonstrations were successful in proving the practicality and reliability of their aircraft.

The Wright brothers' public demonstrations led to contracts with the U.S. Army and European buyers. They established the Wright Company in 1909 to manufacture and sell their airplanes. The company produced both civilian and military aircraft, and the brothers continued to make improvements to their designs. They also trained pilots, establishing one of the first flying schools in the world. The Wright brothers' contributions to aviation were widely recognised, and they received numerous accolades and awards. In 1909, they were awarded the Congressional Gold Medal by the United States government, and they received honours from various international institutions and organisations.

Wilbur Wright's life was cut short when he died of typhoid fever on 30 May 1912, at the age of 45. His death was a significant loss to the field of aviation and to his brother Orville, who continued to work in the aviation industry. Orville sold his interests in the Wright Company in 1915 and retired from active involvement in the business. However, he remained a prominent figure in aviation, serving on various advisory boards and committees. He also continued to advocate for the protection of their patents and the recognition of their contributions to aviation.

Orville Wright lived to see the rapid advancements in aviation technology that followed their pioneering work. He witnessed the development of commercial aviation, the use of airplanes in World War I, and the establishment of airmail services. Orville remained a passionate advocate for aviation and continued to inspire future generations of aviators and engineers. He passed away on 30 January 1948, at the age of 76.

The Wright brothers' legacy is profound and far-reaching. Their invention of the first practical airplane revolutionised transportation and had a lasting impact on the modern world. They demonstrated the importance of systematic experimentation, innovation, and perseverance in achieving technological breakthroughs. Their work laid the foundation for the rapid development of aviation and opened up new possibilities for travel, communication, and commerce.

The Wright brothers' contributions to aviation are commemorated in numerous ways. The Wright brothers' National Memorial in Kitty Hawk, North Carolina, marks the site of their first successful flights. Their original aircraft, the Wright Flyer, is preserved and displayed at the National Air and Space Museum in Washington, D.C. Additionally, their names are honoured in various institutions, awards, and educational programmes dedicated to the advancement of aviation and engineering.

The principles and methods developed by the Wright brothers continue to influence the field of aeronautics. Their emphasis on understanding the underlying physics of flight, their innovative control systems, and their commitment to rigorous testing and improvement remain fundamental to modern aircraft design and engineering. The Wright brothers' story is a testament to the power of human ingenuity and the transformative impact of technological innovation.

The life and achievements of the Wright brothers exemplify the spirit of exploration and the pursuit of knowledge. Their pioneering work in aviation changed the course of history and set the stage for the incredible advancements in flight that followed. The legacy of Wilbur and Orville Wright continues to inspire and guide the future of aviation, reminding us of the limitless possibilities that arise from curiosity, dedication, and innovation.

Albert Sabin

Albert Sabin was born on 26 August 1906 in Białystok, then part of the Russian Empire and now in Poland. His birth name was Abram Saperstein, and he was born into a Jewish family. His early years were marked by the turmoil of World War I and the Russian Revolution, which prompted his family to emigrate to the United States in 1921. They settled in Paterson, New Jersey, where they changed their surname to Sabin. Albert, adapting to his new environment, showed an early interest in science and medicine, inspired by his experiences and the desire to combat the diseases he had witnessed.

Sabin pursued his education with determination, enrolling at New York University to study dentistry but soon switched to medicine. He earned his medical degree in 1931. During his medical studies, Sabin developed a keen interest in infectious diseases, inspired by his professors and the ongoing challenges of combating these illnesses. He decided to specialise in virology and joined the Rockefeller Institute for Medical Research, where he began his lifelong dedication to studying viruses.

In the 1930s, Sabin focused on the study of poliomyelitis, a crippling disease caused by the poliovirus. At that time, polio was a significant public health issue, causing widespread fear and disability. Sabin's research aimed to understand the virus better and develop effective means to combat it. His early work involved studying the behaviour of the poliovirus and its effects on the nervous system. During World War II, Sabin served in the U.S. Army Medical Corps, conducting research on viral diseases affecting soldiers. His work during the war further solidified his expertise in virology and infectious diseases. He investigated diseases such as dengue fever and encephalitis, contributing to the development of vaccines and preventive measures for the military.

After the war, Sabin resumed his research on poliomyelitis at the University of Cincinnati College of Medicine, where he became a prominent figure in the fight against polio. At that time, Jonas Salk had developed the first effective polio vaccine, which used an inactivated (killed) virus to induce immunity. While

Salk's vaccine was a significant breakthrough, Sabin believed that a live, attenuated (weakened) virus vaccine would offer more robust and longer-lasting immunity.

Sabin's approach involved using a weakened form of the poliovirus that could stimulate an immune response without causing the disease. He conducted extensive research and testing to identify strains of the virus that were sufficiently weakened but still capable of inducing immunity. This process involved years of meticulous experimentation and collaboration with other researchers worldwide. By the mid-1950s, Sabin had developed a viable oral polio vaccine (OPV). Unlike Salk's vaccine, which was administered via injection, Sabin's vaccine was taken orally, making it easier to distribute and administer, particularly in mass vaccination campaigns. The oral vaccine also provided intestinal immunity, which helped reduce the spread of the virus.

Sabin's oral polio vaccine underwent extensive field trials, with large-scale studies conducted in the Soviet Union, Eastern Europe, and other regions. These trials demonstrated the vaccine's safety and effectiveness, leading to its widespread adoption. In 1961, the Sabin oral polio vaccine was licensed for use in the United States and many other countries. The vaccine proved to be a game-changer in the fight against polio. Mass immunisation campaigns using the oral polio vaccine led to a dramatic decline in polio cases worldwide. Sabin's vaccine became the cornerstone of global polio eradication efforts, contributing to the near-elimination of the disease. By the late 20th century, polio had been eradicated in most parts of the world, thanks in large part to Sabin's vaccine.

In addition to his work on polio, Sabin made significant contributions to the understanding and prevention of other infectious diseases. He conducted research on toxoplasmosis, a parasitic infection, and contributed to the development of vaccines and treatments for various viral diseases. His work extended beyond the laboratory, as he actively advocated for public health measures and vaccination programs.

Sabin's achievements earned him numerous accolades and recognition. He received the Presidential Medal of Freedom in 1986, one of the highest civilian honours in the United States, in recognition of his contributions to medicine and public health. He also received numerous international awards and honorary degrees from institutions around the world. Despite his successes, Sabin faced challenges and controversies throughout his career. The rivalry between his live vaccine and Salk's killed vaccine sparked debates within the scientific community and among public health officials. However, both vaccines ultimately played crucial roles in the fight against polio, and Sabin's work was widely acknowledged for its impact.

Sabin's dedication to his work extended well into his later years. He continued to research and advocate for vaccination and infectious disease control. In his personal life, Sabin faced tragedy with the loss of his first wife, Sylvia Tregillus, who died of cancer in 1966. He later remarried, and his second wife, Heloisa Sabin, supported his ongoing work and advocacy. Albert Sabin passed away on 3 March 1993 at the age of 86. His legacy lives on through the millions of lives saved and the continued efforts to eradicate polio globally. The Sabin Vaccine Institute, established in his honour, continues to promote vaccine development and public health initiatives worldwide.

Sabin's life and achievements exemplify the profound impact of scientific research and innovation on public health. His relentless pursuit of a more effective polio vaccine transformed the fight against a devastating disease and set the stage for future advancements in vaccine development. Sabin's work underscored the importance of perseverance, collaboration, and a commitment to improving human health.

Albert Sabin's contributions to virology and medicine have left an enduring mark on the world. His oral polio vaccine remains a critical tool in the ongoing effort to eradicate polio, and his legacy continues to inspire researchers and public health professionals. Sabin's dedication to science and his determination to combat infectious diseases serve as a testament to the transformative power of medical research and the enduring quest to protect and improve human health.

Tim Berners-Lee

Tim Berners-Lee was born on 8 June 1955 in London, England. His parents, Mary Lee Woods and Conway Berners-Lee, were both mathematicians and computer scientists who worked on the Ferranti Mark 1, the world's first commercially available general-purpose computer. Growing up in this intellectually stimulating environment, Berners-Lee developed an early interest in electronics and computing. He attended Sheen Mount Primary School and later Emanuel School in London, where he excelled in science and mathematics. He went on to study at Queen's College, Oxford, where he earned a first-class degree in physics in 1976.

After graduating, Berners-Lee worked at Plessey Telecommunications, one of the major telecommunications companies in the UK, where he gained valuable experience in computer networking. In 1980, he began working as an independent contractor at CERN, the European Organisation for Nuclear Research, in Geneva, Switzerland. At CERN, Berners-Lee identified a critical need for a better way to manage and share the vast amounts of information generated by researchers. The complex and distributed nature of the information made it difficult for scientists to access and collaborate efficiently.

Inspired by this problem, Berners-Lee proposed a project based on the concept of hypertext, a method of creating and sharing interlinked documents. He developed a prototype system called ENQUIRE, which allowed researchers to store and retrieve documents linked by hypertext. Although ENQUIRE was limited in scope, it laid the groundwork for Berners-Lee's later work on the World Wide Web. In 1984, he returned to CERN as a fellow, where he continued to refine his ideas about hypertext and information sharing.

In March 1989, Berners-Lee submitted a proposal to his supervisor, Mike Sendall, titled "Information Management: A Proposal." This document outlined a system for managing information using hypertext and a distributed network of computers. Sendall saw potential in the idea and encouraged Berners-Lee to develop it further. By the end of 1990, Berners-Lee had created the fundamental components of the World Wide Web: HTML (HyperText Markup Language), the standard markup language for creating web pages; HTTP (Hypertext Transfer Protocol), the protocol for transmitting data over the web; and the first web browser, called WorldWideWeb, which also served as an editor.

On 20 December 1990, Berners-Lee launched the first website, which was dedicated to providing information about the World Wide Web project. This site explained how to create web pages and set up web servers, effectively serving as a user's guide to the web. The simplicity and flexibility of the system allowed users to link documents and navigate between them easily, revolutionising the way information was shared and accessed.

In 1991, Berners-Lee made the World Wide Web publicly available on the internet, opening it up to a global audience. The web quickly gained traction, with an increasing number of users and websites emerging. To support the growth and development of the web, Berners-Lee founded the World Wide Web Consortium (W3C) in 1994 at the Massachusetts Institute of Technology (MIT). The W3C was established to develop standards and protocols to ensure the long-term growth and interoperability of the web. Under Berners-Lee's leadership, the consortium developed key web standards, including CSS (Cascading Style Sheets) for controlling the presentation of web pages, and XML (eXtensible Markup Language) for structuring data.

Throughout the 1990s and early 2000s, Berners-Lee continued to advocate for an open and accessible web. He emphasised the importance of maintaining the web as a free and open platform, free from commercial and governmental control. His vision for the web was one of universal access to information, fostering collaboration and innovation across diverse fields and communities.

In recognition of his contributions to computer science and the development of the World Wide Web, Berners-Lee received numerous honours and awards. In 2004, he was knighted by Queen Elizabeth II for his pioneering work. He was also awarded the first Millennium Technology Prize by the Finnish Technology Award Foundation in 2004, acknowledging the profound impact of the web on society. Berners-Lee's influence extended beyond his technical achievements. He became a prominent advocate for digital rights, privacy, and net neutrality, arguing that these principles were essential to preserving the web's open and democratic nature. He consistently called for greater transparency and accountability from governments and corporations in their handling of user data and online activity.

In 2009, Berners-Lee founded the World Wide Web Foundation, an organisation dedicated to advancing the open web as a public good and a basic right. The foundation focuses on ensuring affordable access to the web for all, protecting user rights online, and promoting digital literacy. Through this work, Berners-Lee aimed to address the digital divide and ensure that the benefits of the web were shared equitably across the globe.

Berners-Lee's commitment to innovation and social impact continued into the 2010s. In 2012, he joined the UK's Open Data Institute as a co-founder, advocating for the use of open data to drive innovation, improve public services, and promote transparency. The institute works to make data more accessible and usable, fostering a culture of openness and collaboration.

In 2018, Berners-Lee launched a new initiative called Solid, a platform designed to give users greater control over their personal data. Solid aims to decentralise the web by allowing individuals to store their data in personal online data stores (Pods) and choose who can access and use their information. This project reflects Berners-Lee's ongoing commitment to empowering users and protecting privacy in the digital age.

Throughout his career, Berners-Lee remained a vocal advocate for the ethical use of technology and the need to address the societal challenges posed by the digital revolution. He highlighted issues such as misinformation, data breaches, and the concentration of power in the hands of a few tech giants. He argued that these challenges required collective action and a renewed commitment to the principles of openness and collaboration that underpinned the web's creation.

Berners-Lee's contributions to the development of the World Wide Web have had a profound and lasting impact on virtually every aspect of modern life. The web has transformed how people communicate, access information, conduct business, and engage with the world. It has enabled new forms of social interaction, revolutionised industries, and provided a platform for innovation and creativity.

In recognition of his enduring influence, Berners-Lee has received numerous accolades, including the Turing Award in 2016, often referred to as the "Nobel Prize of Computing." This prestigious award honoured his fundamental contributions to the invention of the World Wide Web, the first web browser, and the associated protocols and algorithms.

Despite his remarkable achievements, Berners-Lee has remained humble and dedicated to his vision of an open and accessible web. He continues to inspire new generations of technologists, innovators, and activists to harness the power of the web for the greater good. His work serves as a testament to the transformative potential of technology and the importance of maintaining a commitment to ethical principles and social responsibility.

Tim Berners-Lee's life and achievements exemplify the profound impact that visionary thinking and technical innovation can have on the world. His creation of the World Wide Web revolutionised communication and information sharing, creating a platform that has become an integral part of modern life. His ongoing advocacy for an open and ethical web underscores the importance of preserving the principles that have made the web such a powerful and transformative tool. Berners-Lee's legacy is not only in the technology he created but also in his unwavering commitment to ensuring that the web remains a force for good in the world.

Stephen Hawking

Stephen Hawking was born on 8 January 1942 in Oxford, England. His birth came during World War II, and his parents, Frank and Isobel Hawking, had moved from London to Oxford to escape the bombings. Frank was a research biologist, and Isobel worked as a secretary for a medical research institute. Stephen was the eldest of four children, and his early family life was intellectually stimulating, with discussions at the dinner table often revolving around scientific topics. The family valued education and knowledge, laying a strong foundation for Stephen's future academic pursuits.

Hawking showed an early interest in science and mathematics, although he was not immediately recognised as an exceptional student. He attended St Albans School, where his academic performance was unremarkable, but his natural curiosity and penchant for asking probing questions set him apart. In 1959, at the age of 17, he won a scholarship to study physics at University College, Oxford. His initial years at Oxford were challenging as he found the coursework easy and somewhat boring, leading to a lack of application in his studies. However, he was known for his sharp intellect and often completed his work with minimal effort.

After graduating with a first-class BA degree in physics in 1962, Hawking moved to Cambridge to pursue a PhD in cosmology at Trinity Hall. It was during his time at Cambridge that he began experiencing symptoms of amyotrophic lateral sclerosis (ALS), a neurodegenerative disease. Despite the diagnosis, which gave him only a few years to live, Hawking continued his research with remarkable determination and resilience. His work focused on theoretical physics and cosmology, areas that would come to define his career and contributions to science.

Hawking's early research, under the supervision of Dennis Sciama and later Fred Hoyle, delved into the nature of the universe, particularly black holes. In 1970, he made a groundbreaking discovery known as the second law of black hole dynamics, which stated that the event horizon of a black hole can never decrease in size. This discovery laid the groundwork for further exploration into the relationship between black holes and the laws of thermodynamics.

One of Hawking's most significant contributions to theoretical physics came in 1974 when he proposed that black holes are not completely black but emit radiation, now known as Hawking radiation. This theoretical prediction suggested that black holes could lose mass and eventually evaporate, challenging the previously held notion that nothing could escape from a black hole. Hawking radiation bridged the gap between quantum mechanics and general relativity, two fundamental yet previously incompatible theories of physics. This work not only elevated Hawking's status in the scientific community but also had profound implications for our understanding of the universe.

Despite his worsening physical condition, which eventually left him almost completely paralysed and dependent on a speech-generating device for communication, Hawking's intellectual contributions continued unabated. He became a fellow of the Royal Society in 1974 and was later appointed Lucasian Professor of Mathematics at the University of Cambridge in 1979, a prestigious position once held by Sir Isaac Newton. His research interests expanded to include the nature of singularities, the Big Bang theory, and the unification of general relativity and quantum mechanics.

Hawking's work on the origin and fate of the universe, often conducted in collaboration with other prominent physicists like Roger Penrose, significantly advanced the field of cosmology. The Penrose-Hawking singularity theorems, developed in the late 1960s and early 1970s, demonstrated that singularities—points of infinite density and gravitational pull—are a common feature in general relativity, occurring not only in black holes but also at the beginning of the universe. These theorems provided strong evidence for the Big Bang theory as the origin of the universe.

In addition to his scientific research, Hawking became a best-selling author, bringing complex scientific concepts to a broader audience. His 1988 book, "A Brief History of Time," became an international bestseller, selling over ten million copies and being translated into multiple languages. The book explained fundamental questions about the universe, including the nature of time, the structure of space, and the potential for time travel, in a way that was accessible to the general public. Its success turned Hawking into a global celebrity and a symbol of human resilience and intellectual achievement.

Hawking continued to write and publish throughout his life, authoring several more books that explored the mysteries of the universe. "The Universe in a Nutshell" (2001) and "A Briefer History of Time" (2005, co-authored with Leonard Mlodinow) further elaborated on his theories and the latest developments in cosmology. He also co-wrote a series of children's books with his daughter, Lucy Hawking, introducing younger readers to the wonders of science and the universe.

Hawking's influence extended beyond the scientific and literary communities. He made numerous public appearances, participated in television documentaries, and even guest-starred on popular TV shows like "The Simpsons" and "Star Trek: The Next Generation." His life and work were the subject of the 2014 biographical film "The Theory of Everything," which portrayed his relationship with his first wife, Jane Wilde, and his battle with ALS. Eddie Redmayne's portrayal of Hawking earned him an Academy Award for Best Actor, bringing Hawking's inspirational story to a wide audience.

Throughout his life, Hawking received numerous accolades and awards for his contributions to science. He was appointed a Companion of Honour by Queen Elizabeth II in 1989 and received the Presidential Medal of Freedom, the highest civilian award in the United States, in 2009. Despite these honours, Hawking never won a Nobel Prize, primarily because his most significant theoretical predictions, like Hawking radiation, had not yet been empirically observed.

Hawking's personal life was as complex as his scientific theories. He married Jane Wilde in 1965, and they had three children together: Robert, Lucy, and Timothy. Jane played a crucial role in supporting Hawking through the early years of his illness and his burgeoning career. However, the strains of his physical condition, his increasing fame, and the demands of their family life eventually led to their separation in 1990 and divorce in 1995. Hawking later married Elaine Mason, one of his nurses, in 1995. This marriage also ended in divorce in 2006.

Despite the challenges he faced, Hawking remained active in his scientific and public engagements until his death. He continued to advocate for scientific research and education, often speaking about the importance of understanding and addressing global issues like climate change, artificial intelligence, and the future of humanity. He expressed concerns about the potential risks of AI and the need for ethical guidelines to ensure that technological advancements benefit humanity as a whole.

Hawking's resilience and determination in the face of a debilitating illness inspired millions around the world. His ability to communicate complex scientific ideas in an accessible manner helped bridge the gap between the scientific community and the general public, fostering a greater appreciation for the wonders of the universe. His work has left an indelible mark on the fields of cosmology and theoretical physics, and his legacy continues to influence and inspire new generations of scientists and thinkers.

Stephen Hawking passed away on 14 March 2018, at the age of 76. His death was mourned by people around the globe, from world leaders and renowned scientists to ordinary individuals who had been touched by his work and his story. His ashes were interred in Westminster Abbey, near the graves of Sir Isaac Newton and Charles Darwin, symbolising his monumental contributions to our understanding of the universe.

In reflecting on his life, Hawking once said, "My goal is simple. It is a complete understanding of the universe, why it is as it is and why it exists at all." Through his groundbreaking research and his ability to communicate the mysteries of the cosmos, Stephen Hawking brought us closer to achieving that goal. His life and achievements serve as a testament to the power of the human spirit and the unending quest for knowledge.

Jane Goodall

Jane Goodall was born on 3 April 1934 in London, England, to Mortimer Herbert Morris-Goodall, a businessman, and Margaret Myfanwe Joseph, a novelist. From an early age, Goodall exhibited a keen interest in animals and nature, encouraged by her mother who nurtured her curiosity. Her fascination with the natural world was evident when, at just four years old, she spent hours observing a hen laying an egg. This early experience of patient observation would foreshadow her future career.

In 1952, Goodall completed her schooling at Uplands School in London and then worked as a secretary at Oxford University. Her passion for animals and Africa led her to save money for a trip to Kenya. In 1957, at the age of 23, she finally realised her dream and travelled to Africa, where she met the famous anthropologist and palaeontologist Louis Leakey. Leakey was impressed by her enthusiasm and knowledge of animals and offered her a position as his assistant. Recognising Goodall's potential, Leakey suggested that she study the behaviour of chimpanzees, a task that had never been attempted in such depth before.

In July 1960, Goodall arrived at the Gombe Stream National Park in Tanzania to begin her research. Without any formal scientific training, she faced scepticism from the scientific community. However, her unique approach, characterised by patience and empathy, allowed her to make groundbreaking discoveries. One of her first significant observations was that chimpanzees used tools, a behaviour previously thought to be exclusive to humans. She observed them modifying twigs to fish for termites, challenging the established notion that tool-making was a defining characteristic of humanity.

Goodall's research at Gombe also revealed complex social behaviours among chimpanzees, such as hunting, meat-eating, and social bonding. She documented their intricate social hierarchies, maternal bonds, and even instances of warfare between groups. Her findings revolutionised our understanding of primates and human evolution, demonstrating that chimpanzees exhibit behaviours and emotions strikingly similar to humans.

In 1965, Goodall obtained her PhD in ethology from the University of Cambridge, becoming one of the few individuals to achieve this degree without first having an undergraduate degree. Her thesis, based on her observations at Gombe, was groundbreaking and established her as a leading figure in primatology. She published her first major book, "My Friends the Wild Chimpanzees," in 1969, which brought her work to a broader audience and highlighted the importance of conservation.

Goodall's research also had significant implications for the field of anthropology. Her discoveries challenged the anthropocentric view of human uniqueness and prompted scientists to reconsider the cognitive and emotional capacities of animals. Her work demonstrated the importance of studying animals in their natural habitats, influencing the methodologies of future researchers.

In 1977, Goodall founded the Jane Goodall Institute (JGI) to support the continued research at Gombe and promote conservation efforts. The institute focuses on protecting chimpanzees and their habitats, as well as supporting sustainable development in local communities. Through education and outreach, JGI works to raise awareness about environmental issues and the importance of biodiversity.

Goodall's commitment to conservation extended beyond chimpanzees. She became a global advocate for environmental preservation, travelling extensively to speak about the interconnectedness of all living beings and the need for sustainable practices. Her message emphasised the responsibility of humans to protect the planet and all its inhabitants.

In 1991, Goodall launched the Roots & Shoots program, an initiative aimed at empowering young people to make a positive impact on their communities and the environment. The program encourages youth to engage in projects that promote sustainability, animal welfare, and social justice. Roots & Shoots has grown into a global movement, inspiring young people around the world to take action for a better future.

Throughout her career, Goodall has received numerous accolades and honours for her contributions to science and conservation. She has been awarded the Kyoto Prize, the Benjamin Franklin Medal in Life Science, and the UN Messenger of Peace title, among many others. Her influence extends beyond the scientific community, as she has become a symbol of hope and resilience in the face of environmental challenges.

Goodall's personal life has also been marked by significant events and relationships. She married Dutch photographer Hugo van Lawick in 1964, and they had a son, Hugo Eric Louis, known as "Grub." The couple divorced in 1974, and Goodall later married Derek Bryceson, a Tanzanian parliamentarian and director of Tanzania's national parks, who passed away in 1980. Despite these personal challenges, Goodall's dedication to her work remained unwavering.

Goodall's work has not been without controversy. Her anthropomorphic descriptions of chimpanzees and her empathetic approach to research were initially criticised by some scientists. However, her meticulous documentation and groundbreaking discoveries have earned her widespread respect and admiration. Her holistic perspective on the natural world, combining rigorous scientific research with a deep sense of compassion, has influenced generations of scientists and conservationists.

In recent years, Goodall has continued to travel and speak about environmental issues, advocating for urgent action to address climate change, habitat destruction, and species extinction. She emphasises the importance of individual actions and collective efforts in creating a sustainable future. Goodall's ability to connect with people from diverse backgrounds and inspire them to care for the planet has made her a powerful voice in the environmental movement.

Goodall's legacy extends beyond her scientific contributions. Her life's work has highlighted the importance of empathy, compassion, and respect for all living beings. She has shown that scientific research can coexist with a profound appreciation for the natural world and that individuals can make a difference in protecting the environment.

Jane Goodall's impact on the world is immeasurable. Her pioneering research on chimpanzees has transformed our understanding of primate behaviour and human evolution. Her advocacy for conservation and sustainable development has raised awareness about the urgent need to protect the planet. Through her institute and the Roots & Shoots program, she has empowered countless individuals to take action for a better future. Goodall's life and achievements serve as a testament to the power of curiosity, perseverance, and compassion in making a lasting difference in the world. Her legacy continues to inspire and guide efforts to create a more just and sustainable world for all living beings.

Alan Turing

Alan Turing was born on 23 June 1912 in Maida Vale, London, to Julius Mathison Turing and Ethel Sara Stoney. His father worked for the Indian Civil Service, and his mother came from a family of engineers. From an early age, Turing exhibited remarkable intelligence and a natural inclination towards mathematics and science. He was sent to various schools while his parents were in India, displaying a talent for solving complex problems independently.

Turing attended Sherborne School, a prestigious boarding school, where he continued to demonstrate his exceptional abilities in mathematics and science, despite the school's emphasis on classical studies. He often faced criticism for his unconventional methods and interests, but his passion for scientific inquiry remained undeterred. In 1931, Turing enrolled at King's College, Cambridge, where he studied mathematics. His intellectual prowess quickly became evident, and he graduated with first-class honours in 1934. At Cambridge, he was influenced by the work of John von Neumann and other leading mathematicians, which shaped his future contributions to computer science and cryptography.

In 1936, Turing published his seminal paper, "On Computable Numbers, with an Application to the Entscheidungsproblem." In this work, he introduced the concept of the Turing machine, a theoretical device that could perform any conceivable mathematical computation through a series of simple operations. The Turing machine became a fundamental model for the theory of computation and laid the groundwork for modern computer science. This paper also addressed the Entscheidungsproblem (decision problem) posed by David Hilbert, demonstrating that no general algorithm could solve all mathematical problems, thus proving the limitations of mechanistic computation.

Turing's work caught the attention of Alonzo Church, a prominent American logician, who invited him to Princeton University. Turing spent two years at Princeton, earning a PhD in 1938 under Church's supervision. His dissertation expanded on his earlier work, exploring the mathematical foundations of logic and computation. During his time at Princeton, Turing also developed an interest in cryptography, which would become a critical aspect of his later contributions.

With the outbreak of World War II in 1939, Turing returned to Britain and joined the Government Code and Cypher School at Bletchley Park. He became a key figure in the efforts to break the German Enigma cipher, a formidable encryption device used by the Nazis to secure their communications. Turing's expertise in mathematics and logic proved invaluable in this endeavour. He devised a machine called the Bombe, an electromechanical device designed to expedite the process of deciphering Enigma-encrypted messages. The Bombe significantly increased the efficiency of code-breaking efforts, allowing the Allies to intercept and decode vast amounts of German military communications. This intelligence, known as Ultra, played a crucial role in several Allied victories and is credited with shortening the war by several years.

Turing's contributions to cryptography extended beyond the Enigma machine. He also worked on breaking the Lorenz cipher, used by the German High Command for more strategic communications. His work in this area involved the development of statistical techniques and algorithms that laid the foundation for future advancements in computer science.

Despite his pivotal role in the war effort, Turing's work at Bletchley Park remained classified for many years, and he did not receive public recognition for his contributions during his lifetime. After the war, Turing continued to make significant advancements in the field of computer science. In 1945, he joined the National Physical Laboratory (NPL), where he designed the Automatic Computing Engine (ACE), one of the first designs for a stored-program computer. Although the full-scale ACE was never built due to bureaucratic delays, his detailed design and theoretical work provided critical insights for future computer developments.

In 1948, Turing moved to the University of Manchester, where he worked on the Manchester Mark I, one of the earliest operational stored-program computers. He also developed the concept of artificial intelligence, proposing that machines could be capable of intelligent behaviour. In 1950, he published his famous paper, "Computing Machinery and Intelligence," in which he introduced the Turing Test. This test was designed to determine whether a machine could exhibit behaviour indistinguishable from that of a human. The Turing Test remains a foundational concept in the field of artificial intelligence, sparking ongoing debates and research into the nature of machine intelligence.

Turing's work in biology was equally innovative. He explored the mathematical principles underlying morphogenesis, the process by which organisms develop their shapes and structures. His 1952 paper, "The Chemical Basis of Morphogenesis," proposed that chemical reactions and diffusion processes could explain patterns such as the spots and stripes on animal skins. This work laid the foundation for the field of mathematical biology and influenced subsequent research in developmental biology and pattern formation.

Despite his numerous achievements, Turing's life was marred by personal and legal troubles. In 1952, he was prosecuted for homosexuality, which was then a criminal offence in Britain. He was convicted and given the choice between imprisonment and chemical castration through hormone treatment. Turing chose the latter, a decision that had severe physical and psychological effects on him. His security clearance was revoked, and he was barred from continuing his cryptographic work for the government. This period of his life was marked by intense personal and professional hardship.

Tragically, Turing's life was cut short on 7 June 1954, when he died from cyanide poisoning. His death was ruled a suicide, although some have speculated that it may have been accidental. The circumstances surrounding his death remain a subject of debate. Despite his untimely demise, Turing's legacy endured, and his contributions to mathematics, computer science, cryptography, and artificial intelligence continued to influence future generations of researchers and innovators.

In the decades following his death, Turing's work gradually gained the recognition it deserved. He is now celebrated as one of the most influential figures in the history of computer science and artificial intelligence. In 1966, the Turing Award was established by the Association for Computing Machinery (ACM) to honour individuals who have made significant contributions to the field of computer science. Often regarded as the "Nobel Prize of Computing," the Turing Award remains one of the most prestigious accolades in the discipline.

Public awareness of Turing's contributions also grew, thanks in part to biographies, documentaries, and films that highlighted his achievements and the challenges he faced. The 2014 film "The Imitation Game," starring Benedict Cumberbatch as Turing, brought his story to a global audience, further cementing his legacy as a pioneering scientist and war hero.

In 2009, British Prime Minister Gordon Brown issued an official apology on behalf of the government for the way Turing was treated, acknowledging the profound injustice he suffered. In 2013, Turing was posthumously pardoned by Queen Elizabeth II, recognising his invaluable contributions to the war effort and the field of computer science.

Turing's impact on the modern world is immeasurable. His theoretical and practical work laid the groundwork for the development of modern computers and the field of artificial intelligence. The principles he established continue to guide research in computation, cryptography, and biological modelling. Turing's life and achievements exemplify the profound interplay between scientific curiosity, intellectual rigor, and the human spirit's resilience in the face of adversity.

Alan Turing's legacy is a testament to the power of innovation and the enduring importance of scientific inquiry. His pioneering work has shaped the course of technology and science, influencing countless advancements and applications that define contemporary life. Despite the personal and societal challenges he faced, Turing's contributions have left an indelible mark on history, inspiring future generations to pursue knowledge and innovation with unwavering dedication and courage.

Nelson Mandela

Nelson Mandela was born on 18 July 1918 in the village of Mvezo in Umtata, then part of South Africa's Cape Province. His father, Gadla Henry Mphakanyiswa, was a chief and counsellor to the Thembu royal family, and his mother, Nosekeni Fanny, was the third of his four wives. Mandela's birth name was Rolihlahla, meaning "pulling the branch of a tree" or "troublemaker," and he was later given the name Nelson by his teacher on his first day of primary school, following the custom of giving African children English names. Raised in the Xhosa culture, Mandela was groomed from a young age to assume a leadership role in his community.

Mandela's early education was at a local missionary school, followed by attendance at the Clarkebury Boarding Institute and then Healdtown, a Methodist college. In 1939, he enrolled at the University of Fort Hare, the only residential centre of higher education for black people in South Africa. There, he met Oliver Tambo, who would become a lifelong friend and political ally. Mandela's time at Fort Hare was cut short due to his involvement in a student protest, which led to his expulsion.

In 1941, to avoid an arranged marriage, Mandela fled to Johannesburg, where he worked as a night watchman at a mine before meeting Walter Sisulu, who arranged a job for him at a law firm. During this time, he completed his BA through the University of South Africa and later studied law at the University of the Witwatersrand. In Johannesburg, Mandela became increasingly involved in the struggle against racial oppression and joined the African National Congress (ANC) in 1943.

Mandela, along with Tambo and Sisulu, formed the ANC Youth League in 1944, advocating for a more radical approach to combating racial segregation and discrimination. The Youth League's influence grew, and in 1949, the ANC adopted its Programme of Action, which called for mass resistance, boycotts, strikes, and civil disobedience. Mandela played a key role in these efforts, emerging as a prominent leader in the movement.

The 1950s were marked by heightened activism and increased repression by the apartheid government. Mandela was instrumental in organising the Defiance Campaign of 1952, a nationwide protest against apartheid laws. This campaign led to his arrest and a subsequent nine-month prison sentence, suspended for two years. Despite his legal troubles, Mandela continued his activism and helped draft the Freedom Charter in 1955, a visionary document that called for a non-racial South Africa and equal rights for all citizens.

In 1956, Mandela and 155 other activists were arrested and charged with treason. The trial, which lasted until 1961, ended with all the defendants being acquitted. During this period, Mandela's marriage to his first wife, Evelyn Ntoko Mase, fell apart, and they divorced in 1958. Later that year, he married Winnie Madikizela, who would become a significant figure in the anti-apartheid movement and his life.

As the apartheid regime intensified its repression, Mandela and the ANC adopted more militant tactics. In 1961, he co-founded Umkhonto we Sizwe (Spear of the Nation), the armed wing of the ANC, which carried out acts of sabotage against government installations. In 1962, Mandela secretly left South Africa to garner international support for the anti-apartheid cause and undergo military training. Upon his return, he was arrested and sentenced to five years in prison for leaving the country illegally and inciting workers to strike.

While serving this sentence, Mandela was charged again in what became known as the Rivonia Trial, named after the suburb where the ANC's headquarters were raided. Mandela and his co-defendants faced charges of sabotage, treason, and violent conspiracy. In his famous speech from the dock, Mandela declared his willingness to die for the ideal of a democratic and free society. In 1964, he was sentenced to life imprisonment and sent to Robben Island, where he would spend the next 18 years.

Life on Robben Island was harsh, with prisoners subjected to hard labour, poor living conditions, and limited contact with the outside world. Despite these conditions, Mandela remained a symbol of resistance and hope. He continued to educate himself and his fellow inmates, and his leadership and resolve never wavered. In 1982, he was transferred to Pollsmoor Prison and later to Victor Verster Prison, where he continued to exert influence over the anti-apartheid movement.

During his imprisonment, the global anti-apartheid movement gained momentum. International pressure on the South African government mounted, and calls for Mandela's release grew louder. By the late 1980s, South Africa faced increasing internal unrest and economic sanctions. In 1990, newly elected President F.W. de Klerk announced Mandela's release, a move that marked the beginning of the end for apartheid.

Mandela was released on 11 February 1990, after 27 years in prison. He immediately resumed his leadership role in the ANC and began negotiations with the government to dismantle apartheid. These negotiations were complex and fraught with challenges, including outbreaks of violence and deep-seated mistrust between the parties. Mandela's commitment to reconciliation and his ability to build consensus were crucial in navigating this tumultuous period.

In 1993, Mandela and de Klerk were jointly awarded the Nobel Peace Prize for their efforts to peacefully end apartheid and establish a multiracial democracy. The following year, South Africa held its first democratic elections, in which people of all races could vote. The ANC won a decisive victory, and on 10 May 1994, Mandela was inaugurated as South Africa's first black president. His presidency marked the beginning of a new era in South African history, characterised by efforts to heal the deep wounds of apartheid and build a unified nation.

Mandela's presidency focused on reconciliation, nation-building, and social justice. He established the Truth and Reconciliation Commission, chaired by Archbishop Desmond Tutu, to address the atrocities committed during the apartheid era. The commission aimed to uncover the truth, promote forgiveness, and foster national unity. Mandela also prioritised economic reform, education, and healthcare, seeking to address the vast inequalities that apartheid had entrenched.

Despite the immense challenges, Mandela's leadership and vision inspired a nation and garnered international admiration. He chose not to seek re-election and stepped down in 1999, demonstrating his commitment to democratic principles and the peaceful transfer of power. His successor, Thabo Mbeki, continued many of his policies, but Mandela remained an influential figure in South African and global affairs.

In his post-presidential years, Mandela continued to advocate for peace, justice, and human rights. He established the Nelson Mandela Foundation to promote his legacy and support initiatives aimed at social justice, dialogue, and community building. Mandela also focused on combating HIV/AIDS, a significant issue in South Africa, and worked tirelessly to raise awareness and support for those affected by the disease.

Mandela's personal life was marked by both triumphs and tragedies. His marriage to Winnie Madikizela ended in separation in 1992 and divorce in 1996, amid personal and political strains. In 1998, on his 80th birthday, he married Graça Machel, the widow of Mozambican President Samora Machel. This union brought him great personal happiness and stability in his later years.

Nelson Mandela passed away on 5 December 2013 at the age of 95. His death was met with an outpouring of grief and tributes from around the world. Leaders, dignitaries, and ordinary people paid homage to his life and legacy, recognising his profound impact on the struggle for freedom, equality, and human dignity.

Mandela's legacy is enduring and multifaceted. He is remembered as a freedom fighter, a prisoner of conscience, a unifier, and a statesman. His ability to forgive and his commitment to reconciliation set a powerful example for the world. Mandela's life story, characterised by resilience, humility, and unwavering dedication to justice, continues to inspire people across the globe.

Nelson Mandela's journey from a rural village in South Africa to the presidency and beyond embodies the triumph of the human spirit over adversity. His achievements in dismantling apartheid, fostering reconciliation, and promoting human rights have left an indelible mark on history. Mandela's legacy serves as a reminder of the power of perseverance, compassion, and the relentless pursuit of a more just and equitable world. His life's work continues to resonate, offering hope and inspiration to future generations.

Rosa Parks

Rosa Parks was born on 4 February 1913 in Tuskegee, Alabama, to James and Leona McCauley. Her father was a carpenter, and her mother was a teacher. After her parents separated, Rosa moved with her mother and younger brother to live with her maternal grandparents on a farm in Pine Level, Alabama. Growing up in the racially segregated South, Rosa experienced the harsh realities of racism from an early age. Her grandparents were former slaves and strong advocates for racial equality, which significantly influenced Rosa's outlook on justice and civil rights.

Rosa attended a one-room schoolhouse in Pine Level, which often lacked adequate supplies and resources due to the systemic inequalities imposed by segregation. Despite these challenges, she developed a strong commitment to education. Her mother taught her to read at a young age, and Rosa was an avid student. She later attended the Industrial School for Girls in Montgomery and continued her education at the Alabama State Teachers College for Negroes (now Alabama State University), although she was forced to leave to care for her ill grandmother and subsequently her mother.

In 1932, Rosa married Raymond Parks, a barber and an active member of the National Association for the Advancement of Colored People (NAACP). Raymond's involvement in the NAACP exposed Rosa to civil rights activism and the broader struggle for racial justice. Encouraged by her husband, Rosa became actively involved in the NAACP, joining the Montgomery chapter in 1943. She served as the chapter's secretary, working closely with its president, E.D. Nixon, a prominent civil rights leader. In her role, Rosa investigated cases of racial injustice and helped organise efforts to combat segregation and discrimination.

On 1 December 1955, Rosa Parks' act of defiance against segregation on public buses became a pivotal moment in the Civil Rights Movement. After a long day of work as a seamstress at a department store, she boarded a Montgomery city bus and sat in the "coloured section." When the bus became crowded, the driver demanded that Rosa and three other African American passengers give up their seats for white passengers. Rosa refused to move. Her arrest for violating the city's segregation laws sparked outrage and galvanized the African American community in Montgomery.

Rosa's courageous act led to the Montgomery Bus Boycott, which began on 5 December 1955, the day of her trial. E.D. Nixon and other local leaders formed the Montgomery Improvement Association (MIA) to coordinate the boycott, and they elected a young pastor, Martin Luther King Jr., as its president. The boycott lasted for 381 days, during which African Americans in Montgomery refused to use the city buses, opting instead for carpools, walking, or other means of transportation. Despite facing violence, harassment, and economic hardships, the community remained steadfast in their protest.

The boycott exerted significant economic pressure on the bus company and the city, leading to a legal battle that culminated in a landmark decision. On 13 November 1956, the U.S. Supreme Court ruled in Browder v. Gayle that segregation on public buses was unconstitutional. This victory marked a significant achievement in the struggle for civil rights and highlighted the effectiveness of nonviolent protest and collective action. Rosa Parks became an enduring symbol of resistance and the fight for justice.

Despite the national attention and the success of the boycott, Rosa and her husband faced severe reprisals. Rosa lost her job as a seamstress, and Raymond was forced to leave his job due to the constant harassment they faced. In 1957, the couple moved to Detroit, Michigan, seeking better opportunities and a safer environment. In Detroit, Rosa continued her activism, working alongside prominent civil rights leaders and advocating for racial equality, economic justice, and political empowerment.

Rosa worked for Congressman John Conyers from 1965 to 1988, assisting with constituent services and community outreach. Her role in Conyers' office allowed her to continue her advocacy work and support initiatives aimed at improving the lives of African Americans. Throughout her career, she remained a steadfast advocate for civil rights, participating in numerous marches, rallies, and speaking engagements.

In addition to her work with Conyers, Rosa founded the Rosa and Raymond Parks Institute for Self-Development in 1987, alongside Elaine Eason Steele. The institute aimed to empower young people, particularly African Americans, through educational programs, leadership training, and community service. The "Pathways to Freedom" program, one of the institute's signature initiatives, took young people on educational tours of significant civil rights sites across the country, helping them connect with their heritage and the ongoing struggle for justice.

Rosa received numerous accolades and honors for her contributions to the civil rights movement. She was awarded the NAACP's Spingarn Medal in 1979, the Presidential Medal of Freedom in 1996, and the Congressional Gold Medal in 1999. These recognitions underscored her enduring impact and the profound significance of her actions. Rosa's legacy extended beyond the United States, as she became an international symbol of resistance to oppression and the fight for human rights.

Despite the recognition and accolades, Rosa lived a modest life, always emphasizing that her actions on that December day were a part of a collective struggle for justice. She remained humble and dedicated to the cause of equality, often deflecting personal praise to highlight the broader movement and the countless individuals who contributed to the fight for civil rights.

Rosa's influence reached beyond her lifetime. Her story has been taught in schools, her life commemorated in books, films, and documentaries, and her legacy celebrated through numerous public spaces named in her honor, including Rosa Parks Boulevard in Detroit and the Rosa Parks Museum in Montgomery. Her refusal to give up her seat and the subsequent bus boycott are seen as key moments in the civil rights movement that helped to dismantle institutionalized racism in America.

Rosa's later years were marked by both continued activism and personal challenges. In 1994, she was assaulted in her home by a young intruder, an experience that deeply affected her. However, she remained resilient and continued to advocate for justice and equality. Her health began to decline in the late 1990s, but her spirit and dedication never waned. She passed away on 24 October 2005 at the age of 92. Her death was met with an outpouring of tributes and reflections on her life's work. She lay in honor in the U.S. Capitol Rotunda, the first woman and second African American to receive this distinction, underscoring the profound impact of her contributions to American society.

Rosa Parks' life and achievements stand as a testament to the power of individual courage and collective action in the fight for justice. Her refusal to surrender her bus seat sparked a movement that transformed the American civil rights landscape. Through her unwavering commitment to equality, she inspired generations to challenge injustice and strive for a more inclusive and equitable world. Her legacy continues to resonate, reminding us of the enduring importance of standing up for what is right, even in the face of adversity. Rosa Parks remains a symbol of dignity, strength, and the unyielding pursuit of justice, her life story a beacon of hope and a call to action for all who seek to make a difference in the world.

Henry Ford

Henry Ford was born on 30 July 1863 on a farm in Greenfield Township, Michigan, to William and Mary Ford. His father was an immigrant from Ireland, and his mother was the daughter of Belgian immigrants. From a young age, Ford displayed a keen interest in mechanics and engineering, often disassembling and reassembling watches and machinery. This curiosity and hands-on approach to learning laid the foundation for his future innovations in the automotive industry.

At the age of 16, Ford left the family farm to work as an apprentice machinist in Detroit. He gained valuable experience working at James F. Flower & Bros. and later at the Detroit Dry Dock Company. During this time, he developed a deep understanding of steam engines and other mechanical systems. In 1882, Ford returned to the farm, but his interest in machinery never waned. He soon took a job with the Westinghouse Engine Company, where he serviced steam engines. This position further honed his technical skills and introduced him to the emerging field of internal combustion engines.

In 1888, Ford married Clara Bryant, and they settled on a farm in Detroit. He continued to work on improving engines and machinery, eventually securing a position as chief engineer at the Edison Illuminating Company in 1891. Ford's work at Edison provided him with the financial stability and resources to pursue his passion for automotive engineering. He began experimenting with gasoline engines, culminating in the creation of his first gasoline-powered vehicle, the Quadricycle, in 1896. The success of the Quadricycle convinced Ford to devote himself to the development of automobiles.

In 1899, Ford co-founded the Detroit Automobile Company with backing from local investors. However, the company faced numerous challenges, including high production costs and mechanical failures. The venture ultimately failed, but Ford's determination remained unshaken. He continued to refine his designs and seek new opportunities. In 1903, Ford and a group of investors founded the Ford Motor Company. This time, Ford's persistence and innovative spirit paid off. The company introduced the Model A, which was well-received but still relatively expensive and limited in production.

Ford's breakthrough came in 1908 with the introduction of the Model T. The Model T was affordable, reliable, and easy to maintain, making it accessible to a broad segment of the population. Its success was unprecedented, revolutionising personal transportation and transforming the automotive industry. The key to the Model T's affordability lay in Ford's innovative manufacturing techniques. He implemented assembly line production, which drastically reduced the time and cost of manufacturing. This method allowed the company to produce cars quickly and efficiently, making the Model T even more affordable for consumers.

The introduction of the moving assembly line in 1913 further revolutionised manufacturing. Inspired by techniques used in the meatpacking industry, Ford developed a system where workers remained stationary while the product moved along a conveyor belt. This innovation increased production speed, reduced labour costs, and improved product consistency. By 1914, Ford was producing more than 300,000 Model Ts annually, a feat previously unimaginable in the automotive industry.

Ford's manufacturing innovations extended beyond the assembly line. He believed in paying his workers well to ensure a motivated and stable workforce. In 1914, he introduced the $5 workday, which doubled the average wage for factory workers. This policy not only reduced employee turnover and increased productivity but also enabled workers to afford the cars they were producing. Ford's commitment to improving working conditions and wages earned him a reputation as a progressive employer.

The success of the Model T made Ford a household name and established the Ford Motor Company as a dominant force in the automotive industry. By the 1920s, more than half of the cars in the United States were Model Ts. Ford's influence extended beyond the automotive industry, shaping American society and culture. The widespread availability of affordable automobiles transformed the way people lived and worked, facilitating urbanisation, suburbanisation, and economic growth.

Despite his success, Ford faced numerous challenges and controversies. He was a staunch opponent of labour unions, believing they interfered with his vision of harmonious employer-employee relations. This opposition led to significant labour disputes, including the infamous Battle of the Overpass in 1937, where Ford security personnel clashed with union organisers. Ford's reputation was further tarnished by his publication of anti-Semitic articles in his newspaper, The Dearborn Independent. These articles promoted conspiracy theories and harmful stereotypes, drawing widespread criticism and condemnation. In 1927, Ford issued a public apology and retracted the articles, but the damage to his reputation lingered.

During the Great Depression, Ford faced financial difficulties as sales declined and competition increased. However, his company played a crucial role in supporting the war effort during World War II. Ford Motor Company converted its production facilities to manufacture military vehicles, aircraft engines, and other wartime equipment. The company's contribution to the war effort was significant, underscoring Ford's ability to adapt and innovate in times of crisis.

In the post-war years, Ford's influence began to wane as new management took over the company. His grandson, Henry Ford II, assumed control of the company in 1945 and implemented significant changes to modernise and revitalise the business. Despite stepping back from day-to-day operations, Henry Ford remained a prominent figure and continued to shape the company's direction until his death.

Henry Ford passed away on 7 April 1947 at the age of 83. His legacy is marked by his contributions to industrial innovation, manufacturing, and the transformation of American society. Ford's pioneering use of assembly line production revolutionised manufacturing processes across industries, setting new standards for efficiency and productivity. His commitment to paying fair wages and improving working conditions set a precedent for labour relations and corporate responsibility.

Ford's impact on the automotive industry is undeniable. The Model T remains an iconic symbol of the early 20th century, representing the democratization of personal transportation and the rise of consumer culture. Ford's vision of making cars accessible to the masses reshaped the automotive landscape and laid the foundation for the modern automobile industry.

Beyond his industrial achievements, Ford's philanthropic efforts and contributions to education and research also left a lasting mark. He established the Ford Foundation in 1936 to support various charitable initiatives, including education, scientific research, and public welfare. The foundation remains one of the largest and most influential philanthropic organisations in the world, continuing Ford's legacy of giving back to society.

Ford's life was a complex interplay of innovation, ambition, and controversy. While he is celebrated for his contributions to industrialisation and the automotive industry, his legacy is also marred by his opposition to labour unions and his promotion of anti-Semitic views. Nevertheless, his impact on manufacturing, transportation, and American society is profound and enduring.

Henry Ford's life and achievements reflect the transformative power of innovation and the enduring influence of visionary leadership. His pioneering work in automotive manufacturing revolutionised industry practices and made personal transportation accessible to millions. Despite facing numerous challenges and controversies, Ford's legacy as a titan of industry and a catalyst for social change endures, shaping the course of modern history and continuing to inspire future generations of innovators and entrepreneurs.

Florence Nightingale

Florence Nightingale was born on 12 May 1820 in Florence, Italy, to William Edward Nightingale and Frances Nightingale. Her family belonged to the affluent British upper class, and she was named after the city of her birth. Florence's father was a wealthy landowner who ensured she received an extensive education, which was uncommon for women at the time. She studied history, mathematics, philosophy, and various languages. From a young age, Florence felt a strong calling to serve humanity, which she identified as a divine calling to become a nurse.

Despite her family's opposition, Florence pursued her nursing vocation. At 24, she defied societal expectations and began her training at the Institution of Protestant Deaconesses in Kaiserswerth, Germany, in 1844. This experience solidified her commitment to nursing, and she later worked in Paris with the Sisters of Mercy. Upon returning to England, she took a position as Superintendent of the Institution for the Care of Sick Gentlewomen in London, a role she excelled in due to her dedication and organisational skills.

The outbreak of the Crimean War in 1853 marked a turning point in Nightingale's career. Reports of appalling conditions for wounded soldiers reached England, prompting Nightingale to volunteer her services. In 1854, she was appointed to oversee a team of 38 nurses at the military hospital in Scutari, Turkey. Upon arrival, Nightingale was appalled by the unsanitary conditions, lack of supplies, and inadequate care. Determined to improve the situation, she implemented strict hygiene practices, secured essential supplies, and reorganised the hospital's structure.

Nightingale's efforts drastically reduced the mortality rate among wounded soldiers. Her dedication earned her the nickname "The Lady with the Lamp," as she was known for making rounds at night to check on her patients. Her work during the Crimean War not only saved countless lives but also brought significant attention to the importance of nursing and sanitary conditions in hospitals. Upon her return to England in 1856, Nightingale was hailed as a national hero.

Determined to reform healthcare, Nightingale used her newfound fame and influence to advocate for change. She presented her findings from the Crimean War to the Royal Commission on the Health of the Army, highlighting the critical need for sanitary reform in military and civilian hospitals. Her detailed statistical analysis and persuasive arguments led to significant improvements in sanitary practices, both in the military and in public health systems.

In 1860, Nightingale founded the Nightingale Training School for Nurses at St. Thomas' Hospital in London. This institution marked the beginning of professional nursing education, setting high standards for nursing practice and training. The school emphasised the importance of practical experience, discipline, and compassionate care. Graduates of the Nightingale Training School went on to establish nursing schools worldwide, spreading Nightingale's principles and significantly raising the standards of nursing care.

Nightingale's contributions extended beyond direct patient care and nursing education. She was an accomplished statistician, using data to advocate for public health reforms. Her pioneering use of statistical graphics, including the polar area diagram (also known as the Nightingale Rose Diagram), effectively communicated the impact of sanitary conditions on health outcomes. This innovative approach to data visualisation helped to persuade policymakers and the public of the need for sanitary reforms.

Throughout her life, Nightingale continued to write extensively on health care, sanitation, and nursing. Her seminal work, "Notes on Nursing: What It Is and What It Is Not," published in 1860, became a foundational text for the nursing profession. In this book, she outlined essential principles of nursing care, emphasising the importance of hygiene, observation, and compassionate patient care. Her writings influenced generations of nurses and healthcare professionals, shaping the development of modern nursing.

Despite suffering from chronic illness later in life, Nightingale remained actively involved in healthcare reform. She corresponded with international health leaders, provided guidance on hospital design and sanitation, and continued to advocate for public health improvements. Her efforts contributed to significant advancements in healthcare systems in Britain and around the world.

Nightingale's achievements were recognised with numerous honours and awards. In 1883, she was awarded the Royal Red Cross by Queen Victoria. In 1907, she became the first woman to receive the Order of Merit, one of Britain's highest civilian honours. Her legacy was further immortalised through the establishment of the Florence Nightingale Medal by the International Committee of the Red Cross, awarded to outstanding nurses and healthcare workers globally.

Florence Nightingale passed away on 13 August 1910 at the age of 90. Her death marked the end of an extraordinary life dedicated to the service of others and the transformation of healthcare. Nightingale's impact on nursing and public health is immeasurable. She elevated the status of nursing from a lowly regarded occupation to a respected profession, grounded in scientific principles and compassionate care. Her emphasis on sanitation, hygiene, and evidence-based practice revolutionised healthcare, saving countless lives and improving health outcomes worldwide.

Nightingale's legacy continues to inspire and guide the nursing profession. Her commitment to patient care, rigorous training, and public health advocacy set the standard for modern nursing. The principles she championed remain central to nursing education and practice, underscoring the enduring relevance of her contributions. Florence Nightingale's life and achievements exemplify the power of dedication, compassion, and innovation in transforming healthcare and improving the lives of people around the world. Her legacy serves as a testament to the profound impact one individual can have on the well-being of humanity, and her contributions continue to resonate in the field of nursing and beyond.

Neil Armstrong

Neil Armstrong was born on 5 August 1930 in Wapakoneta, Ohio, to Stephen Koenig Armstrong and Viola Louise Engel. His fascination with aviation began early, influenced by his father, who took him to the Cleveland Air Races. Armstrong's first flight was at the age of six, sparking a lifelong passion for flying. He earned his pilot's licence before his driver's licence and was determined to pursue a career in aviation.

Armstrong attended Blume High School and then went on to study aeronautical engineering at Purdue University on a Navy scholarship. His education was interrupted in 1949 when he was called to serve in the Korean War. As a naval aviator, he flew 78 combat missions, demonstrating his skill and bravery. After the war, he returned to Purdue, completing his degree in 1955. He married Janet Shearon in 1956, and they had three children together: Eric, Karen, and Mark. Armstrong's career took off when he became a test pilot for the National Advisory Committee for Aeronautics (NACA), the precursor to NASA.

As a test pilot at Edwards Air Force Base, Armstrong flew the X-15 rocket plane, pushing the boundaries of high-speed and high-altitude flight. He flew over 200 different models of aircraft, including jets, rockets, helicopters, and gliders. His work was dangerous and demanding, but it was excellent preparation for his future role as an astronaut. Armstrong's calm demeanor and technical expertise made him a standout candidate for NASA's astronaut program.

In 1962, Armstrong was selected as part of NASA's second group of astronauts. His first space mission was as command pilot of Gemini 8 in 1966. During this mission, Armstrong performed the first successful docking of two spacecraft in orbit, but the mission nearly ended in disaster when a thruster malfunctioned, causing the spacecraft to spin uncontrollably. Armstrong's quick thinking and calm response saved the crew and spacecraft, bringing them back to safety.

Armstrong's skills and experience made him the ideal choice to command Apollo 11, the first manned mission to land on the Moon. On 16 July 1969, Apollo 11 launched from Kennedy Space Center with Armstrong, Edwin "Buzz" Aldrin, and Michael Collins on board. After a three-day journey, the lunar module, Eagle, separated from the command module, Columbia, and descended to the Moon's surface. On 20 July 1969, Armstrong and Aldrin landed on the Moon while Collins orbited above.

As Armstrong descended the ladder of the lunar module, he spoke the famous words, "That's one small step for man, one giant leap for mankind." These words marked humanity's first steps on another celestial body. Armstrong spent about two and a half hours exploring the lunar surface with Aldrin, collecting samples, conducting experiments, and taking photographs. The successful landing and return of Apollo 11 fulfilled President Kennedy's goal of landing a man on the Moon and returning him safely to Earth, set eight years earlier.

The Apollo 11 mission was a monumental achievement, showcasing the capabilities of human ingenuity, engineering, and determination. Armstrong's role as the first man to walk on the Moon made him an international hero and a symbol of American space exploration. He received numerous awards and honors, including the Presidential Medal of Freedom, the Congressional Space Medal of Honor, and the Congressional Gold Medal.

After Apollo 11, Armstrong continued to contribute to NASA and the field of aerospace. He served as Deputy Associate Administrator for Aeronautics at NASA Headquarters in Washington, D.C., before leaving NASA in 1971 to become a professor of aerospace engineering at the University of Cincinnati. Armstrong valued education and sought to inspire future generations of engineers and scientists. He taught at the university for nearly a decade, sharing his knowledge and experiences with students.

Armstrong also served on several corporate boards and participated in various investigations and commissions, including the Rogers Commission, which investigated the Challenger disaster in 1986. His technical expertise and reputation for integrity made him a respected voice in aerospace and engineering circles. Despite his fame, Armstrong was known for his humility and preference for privacy. He rarely sought the spotlight and was modest about his achievements, often emphasizing the collective effort of the Apollo program and the thousands of people who made the Moon landing possible.

In his later years, Armstrong continued to advocate for space exploration and remained engaged with developments in aerospace. He made occasional public appearances, giving speeches and participating in anniversary events related to the Apollo missions. His legacy as a pioneer of space exploration remained strong, inspiring new generations of astronauts and engineers.

Armstrong passed away on 25 August 2012 at the age of 82 due to complications from heart surgery. His death was met with tributes from around the world, recognizing his contributions to space exploration and his role as a symbol of human achievement. President Barack Obama described him as one of the greatest American heroes, and tributes poured in from NASA, fellow astronauts, world leaders, and admirers.

Neil Armstrong's legacy is firmly embedded in the history of space exploration. His "small step" on the Moon represented a giant leap in humanity's quest to explore the cosmos. His achievements demonstrated the potential of human ingenuity and the importance of perseverance, teamwork, and dedication. Armstrong's life and career continue to inspire those who dream of exploring the unknown and pushing the boundaries of what is possible.

Armstrong's influence extends beyond his achievements in space. He exemplified qualities of leadership, humility, and a commitment to advancing knowledge and exploration. His dedication to education and his contributions to aerospace engineering have left a lasting impact on the field. As humanity looks towards future missions to the Moon, Mars, and beyond, Armstrong's legacy serves as a reminder of the remarkable achievements that can be accomplished through vision, hard work, and collaboration.

Neil Armstrong's life was a testament to the spirit of exploration and the pursuit of excellence. His journey from a small town in Ohio to the surface of the Moon is a story of passion, perseverance, and pioneering achievement. As the first human to set foot on another world, Armstrong's legacy will endure for generations, symbolizing the boundless possibilities of space exploration and human ingenuity.

Catherine the Great

Catherine the Great, born Sophie Friederike Auguste von Anhalt-Zerbst on 2 May 1729 in Stettin, Prussia (now Szczecin, Poland), was destined to become one of Russia's most significant and influential rulers. Her father, Christian August, was a minor German prince, and her mother, Johanna Elisabeth of Holstein-Gottorp, had ambitions for her daughter's rise to prominence. Sophie's early education was rigorous, focused on French, literature, philosophy, and history, which equipped her with a keen intellect and an enlightened worldview.

In 1744, Sophie was invited to Russia by Empress Elizabeth, who was looking for a bride for her nephew and heir, Grand Duke Peter of Holstein-Gottorp. Sophie converted to Eastern Orthodoxy, changed her name to Catherine (Yekaterina) and married Peter in 1745. The marriage was troubled from the start, with Peter displaying little interest in ruling and even less in his wife. Catherine, however, was determined and ambitious, immersing herself in Russian culture and politics. She cultivated alliances with key political figures and members of the Russian court.

Peter III ascended to the throne in January 1762, but his erratic policies and pro-Prussian sympathies quickly alienated many, including the military and the nobility. Catherine, sensing an opportunity, conspired with her supporters to overthrow her husband. In July 1762, a coup was staged, and Peter was forced to abdicate. He was subsequently imprisoned and mysteriously died shortly thereafter, leaving Catherine to be crowned as Empress of Russia.

Catherine's reign marked a period of significant reform and expansion for Russia. She was a proponent of the Enlightenment and corresponded with prominent intellectuals such as Voltaire, Diderot, and Montesquieu. These interactions influenced her policies and reforms, although she often faced resistance from the traditional Russian aristocracy. One of her primary goals was to modernise Russia and bring it in line with Western European nations.

She sought to reform the administration of the government, improve the legal system, and promote education and the arts.

In 1767, Catherine convened the Legislative Commission, an assembly aimed at reviewing and modernising the Russian legal code. Although the commission was ultimately dissolved without achieving its goals, it was a significant step towards reform and demonstrated Catherine's commitment to rational governance. She issued the "Nakaz" or "Instruction," a document outlining her vision for a just and enlightened legal system based on the principles of equality and the rule of law.

Catherine's reign was also marked by extensive territorial expansion. She successfully waged wars against the Ottoman Empire, securing access to the Black Sea and gaining control over Crimea, thereby strengthening Russia's southern borders and its influence in the region. These victories not only enhanced Russia's strategic position but also boosted Catherine's prestige. Additionally, under her rule, Russia participated in the partitions of Poland, which resulted in substantial territorial gains and the integration of millions of new subjects into the Russian Empire.

Domestically, Catherine focused on strengthening the power of the nobility to secure their support for her rule. She issued the Charter to the Nobility in 1785, which codified the privileges of the Russian aristocracy, granting them greater autonomy over their lands and exempting them from certain taxes and military service. This move helped to stabilise her reign by ensuring the loyalty of the influential noble class.

Catherine was also a patron of the arts and education. She founded the Smolny Institute for Noble Maidens, the first state-funded institution for the education of women in Russia. Her patronage extended to the arts, literature, and sciences, and she played a significant role in the cultural development of Russia. The Hermitage Museum, one of the largest and most prestigious museums in the world, began as Catherine's private art collection. She amassed a vast collection of paintings, sculptures, and other works of art, making St. Petersburg a cultural centre of Europe.

Despite her enlightened ideals, Catherine's reign was not without its challenges and contradictions. While she sought to modernise Russia and improve the lives of her subjects, she also faced significant resistance to her reforms. The Pugachev Rebellion of 1773-1775, led by Yemelyan Pugachev, a Cossack who claimed to be Peter III, was a significant uprising of serfs and Cossacks against her rule. The rebellion exposed the deep social and economic divisions within Russian society and the widespread discontent among the peasantry. Catherine responded with a brutal crackdown, and the rebellion was suppressed, but it highlighted the limitations of her reforms and the ongoing struggles within Russian society.

Catherine's personal life was as dynamic and complex as her political career. She had numerous lovers, many of whom were influential political figures and military leaders. These relationships often benefited her politically, as she skillfully navigated court intrigues and alliances. Her most notable relationship was with Grigory Potemkin, a military leader and statesman who played a crucial role in her southern campaigns and the colonisation of newly acquired territories.

Throughout her reign, Catherine maintained a delicate balance between reform and tradition, navigating the complex political landscape of the Russian Empire. Her ability to adapt and respond to the changing circumstances of her time was a testament to her political acumen and resilience. She was a ruler of immense ambition and vision, dedicated to transforming Russia into a modern, enlightened state.

Catherine the Great died on 17 November 1796, after suffering a stroke. She was succeeded by her son, Paul I, whose reign was marked by attempts to reverse many of her policies. Despite the challenges and contradictions of her rule, Catherine left a lasting legacy as one of Russia's greatest and most influential monarchs. Her reign marked a period of significant territorial expansion, cultural development, and administrative reform, which laid the foundations for Russia's emergence as a major European power. Her life and achievements continue to be studied and admired, reflecting the enduring impact of her remarkable leadership.

Rosalind Franklin

Rosalind Franklin, born on 25 July 1920 in London, was an exceptional scientist whose contributions to the understanding of molecular structures, particularly DNA, have had a profound impact on biology and medicine. Raised in a well-to-do, intellectually stimulating family, she was destined for academic excellence. Her father, Ellis Franklin, was a well-known banker and educator who championed women's education, and her mother, Muriel, supported her children's intellectual pursuits. Despite some family reservations about women in science, Rosalind's ambition was unwavering.

Franklin attended St Paul's Girls' School, where she excelled in science and Latin, before enrolling at Newnham College, Cambridge in 1938. Here, she focused on physical chemistry and graduated in 1941. During World War II, she worked as a research assistant at the British Coal Utilisation Research Association, investigating the porosity of coal, which led to her PhD in 1945. Her work on the microstructure of carbon and coal was highly regarded and pivotal for her career, illustrating her capability to marry theoretical insights with practical applications.

In 1947, Franklin moved to Paris to work with Jacques Mering at the Laboratoire Central des Services Chimiques de l'État. Here, she refined her expertise in X-ray crystallography, a technique vital for understanding molecular structures. Her time in Paris was transformative, as she developed not only her scientific skills but also a deep appreciation for French culture and intellectual life. By the time she returned to London in 1951 to work at King's College, she was a formidable scientist.

At King's College London, Franklin was assigned to work on DNA. Her colleague Maurice Wilkins initially misunderstood her role, leading to a tense relationship. Despite this, Franklin made critical advancements in understanding DNA's structure. She used X-ray diffraction to produce clear images of DNA, including the famous Photograph 51, which revealed the helical structure of DNA. Her meticulous approach and rigorous analysis provided the empirical foundation that James Watson and Francis Crick used to build their double helix model of DNA in 1953. Franklin's work was pivotal, yet she was not immediately credited for her contributions, partly due to the competitive and often secretive nature of scientific research at the time.

Frustrated by the working conditions and interpersonal conflicts at King's College, Franklin accepted a position at Birkbeck College in 1953, where she was able to focus on the structure of viruses. Her work on the tobacco mosaic virus was groundbreaking. She demonstrated that RNA within the virus was a single-strand helix, providing insight into viral structure and replication. Her research significantly advanced the field of virology and laid the groundwork for future discoveries about virus behaviour and structure.

Despite her career being cut tragically short by ovarian cancer, Franklin continued to work diligently. Even while undergoing treatment, she published 19 papers on viruses, leaving an indelible mark on the scientific community. Her colleagues, particularly Aaron Klug, who would later win a Nobel Prize, continued her work on viruses, building on the foundation she had established.

Rosalind Franklin's legacy extends beyond her scientific achievements. She was a trailblazer for women in science, working in an era when female scientists faced significant barriers. Her determination, intellectual rigor, and refusal to let gender biases impede her work set a powerful example. Though not widely recognised during her lifetime, Franklin's contributions to science were immense and essential. Her meticulous research methods and groundbreaking discoveries have had lasting impacts, particularly in our understanding of the molecular structures that are fundamental to life itself.

In the years following her death on 16 April 1958, Franklin's role in the discovery of DNA's structure became more widely acknowledged. Her contributions have been recognised through numerous posthumous honours, including buildings named after her, awards in her honour, and a growing appreciation for the pivotal role she played in one of the most important scientific discoveries of the 20th century. Her life and work continue to inspire new generations of scientists, both male and female, to pursue rigorous, innovative research and to challenge the barriers that they may face in their own careers.

Rosalind Franklin's story is a testament to her remarkable intellect, resilience, and passion for science. Her contributions to our understanding of DNA and viruses remain foundational, and her legacy as a pioneering woman in science is celebrated more than ever today. Through her unwavering dedication to scientific inquiry and her exceptional achievements, Franklin not only advanced human knowledge but also paved the way for future generations of scientists.

Ada Lovelace

Ada Lovelace, born Augusta Ada Byron on December 10, 1815, in London, was a pioneering figure in the history of computing. Her father was the renowned poet Lord Byron, and her mother, Annabella Milbanke, was a highly educated and mathematically inclined woman. Despite separating shortly after Ada's birth, Annabella ensured that Ada received an extensive education, especially in mathematics and science, hoping to prevent any influence of her father's perceived madness. This decision proved to be crucial in shaping Ada's future contributions to the field of computing

From an early age, Ada showed a remarkable aptitude for mathematics and logic. Her education was rigorous and included tutoring from prominent figures such as Mary Somerville, one of the leading scientific authors of the time. Under Somerville's mentorship, Ada's fascination with mathematics grew, and she developed a keen interest in mechanical engineering and the possibilities of machines.

In 1833, Ada was introduced to Charles Babbage, a mathematician and inventor, through Mary Somerville. Babbage was working on his Difference Engine, an early mechanical computer designed to perform mathematical calculations. Ada was captivated by Babbage's work and the potential of his machines. She and Babbage developed a close intellectual relationship, exchanging ideas and insights about mathematics and engineering. Ada's understanding of Babbage's concepts was profound, and she quickly became one of the few people who could grasp the full implications of his inventions.

Babbage's next project, the Analytical Engine, was a more advanced mechanical computer capable of performing any calculation or algorithm. In 1842, Italian mathematician Luigi Federico Menabrea published a paper describing the Analytical Engine, which Ada translated from French to English at Babbage's request. However, Ada didn't just translate the paper; she also added her own extensive notes, which ended up being three times longer than the original text. These notes, published in 1843, contained what is now considered the first algorithm intended to be processed by a machine, making Ada Lovelace the world's first computer programmer.

Ada's notes demonstrated her visionary understanding of the Analytical Engine's potential beyond mere calculation. She foresaw that such a machine could go beyond number-crunching to manipulate symbols and even create music, anticipating the modern concept of general-purpose computing. She articulated the idea that machines could be programmed to perform tasks following a sequence of operations, a fundamental principle of computer science. Her insight that computers could operate on abstract symbols and be used for tasks such as composing music, not just for arithmetic calculations, was revolutionary and ahead of her time.

Despite her remarkable intellect and contributions, Ada's ideas were not widely recognised during her lifetime. The scientific community largely overlooked her work, partly due to the societal attitudes towards women in science and technology at the time. Additionally, Ada's health was fragile throughout her life, and she struggled with various illnesses. She married William King in 1835, who later became the Earl of Lovelace, making Ada the Countess of Lovelace. They had three children together. Despite her domestic responsibilities and health issues, Ada continued to pursue her intellectual interests and corresponded with other leading scientists and mathematicians.

Ada Lovelace's life was also marked by a series of personal challenges and tragedies. She was known for her high spirits and sometimes erratic behaviour, which led to periods of ill health. Ada became involved in various scientific ventures and even attempted to create a mathematical model for gambling, which led to financial difficulties. She sought to apply her mathematical expertise to practical and theoretical problems, always pushing the boundaries of her knowledge and capabilities.

Tragically, Ada Lovelace's life was cut short when she died of uterine cancer on November 27, 1852, at the age of 36. Her contributions to computing remained largely unrecognised until the mid-20th century, when her work was rediscovered by scholars and historians of computing. The recognition of her achievements has since grown, and she is now celebrated as a pioneer who laid the groundwork for modern computing.

Ada Lovelace's legacy extends beyond her technical contributions to her role as a visionary who saw the broader implications of computing. She represents the intersection of the arts and sciences, embodying the idea that creativity and analytical thinking are not mutually exclusive but can complement each other. Her life and work have inspired countless individuals, particularly women, to pursue careers in science, technology, engineering, and mathematics (STEM).

Today, Ada Lovelace is honoured in various ways, including the naming of the Ada programming language after her and the celebration of Ada Lovelace Day, which promotes the achievements of women in STEM fields. Her contributions to the early concepts of computing have earned her a place as a foundational figure in the history of technology. The recognition she receives now highlights the importance of her work and the enduring impact of her visionary ideas on the field of computer science.

Ada Lovelace's life was one of intellectual brilliance, visionary thinking, and pioneering contributions to the field of computing. Her collaboration with Charles Babbage and her development of the first algorithm intended for a machine laid the foundations for modern computer programming. Despite the challenges she faced, including societal biases and personal health struggles, Ada's legacy endures as a testament to her extraordinary contributions and the lasting influence of her work on the world of technology.

Louis Braille

Louis Braille was born on 4 January 1809 in Coupvray, a small village near Paris, France. His father, Simon-René Braille, was a harness maker, and Louis spent much of his early childhood in his father's workshop. At the age of three, while playing with some of his father's tools, Louis accidentally injured his eye with an awl, leading to a severe infection that eventually spread to both eyes, rendering him completely blind by the age of five. Despite this setback, Louis showed a remarkable intellect and determination from a young age.

His parents, recognising his potential, were determined to provide him with an education. At first, Louis attended the local school, where he learned by listening and memorising the lessons. However, recognising the limitations of his education in a typical school setting, his parents enrolled him at the Royal Institute for Blind Youth in Paris when he was ten years old. This institution was one of the first schools for blind children in the world and offered a chance for Louis to receive a more specialised education.

At the Institute, conditions were harsh, and the methods of instruction were rudimentary. Students read by tracing raised letters with their fingers, a method that was slow and cumbersome. Despite these challenges, Louis excelled in his studies, particularly in music and mathematics. He was a talented musician, learning to play the cello and the organ, and his musical skills later provided him with a means of earning a livelihood.

In 1821, Charles Barbier, a former French army captain, visited the Institute to demonstrate his system of night writing. This system, designed for soldiers to communicate silently and without light, used a series of raised dots and dashes to represent sounds. While Barbier's system was innovative, it was also complex and difficult to master. Recognising its potential, Louis began to experiment with ways to simplify and improve it.

By the age of fifteen, Louis had developed his own system of raised dots that could be easily felt with the fingertips. His system used a six-dot cell to represent letters, numbers, and punctuation, which allowed for a simple yet versatile method of reading and writing. Each cell could represent 64 different characters based on the arrangement of the dots. This system was revolutionary, providing a practical means for blind individuals to read and write independently.

Louis's system was met with resistance from the authorities at the Institute and from the broader society. Many were sceptical of its practicality and reluctant to adopt a new method of teaching. However, Louis persisted in promoting his invention, teaching it to his fellow students and refining it over the years. His system began to gain acceptance among the students, who found it far superior to the embossed letter system.

In 1829, Louis published his first book explaining his system, titled "Method of Writing Words, Music, and Plain Songs by Means of Dots, for Use by the Blind and Arranged for Them." This publication marked a significant milestone in his efforts to promote his invention. However, widespread acceptance was still slow, and it wasn't until after his death that his system gained official recognition.

In addition to developing his system for reading and writing, Louis Braille also adapted it for use in musical notation. This adaptation enabled blind musicians to read and compose music, further enhancing their ability to participate fully in the musical arts. His work in this area was groundbreaking and opened up new opportunities for blind musicians.

Despite his achievements, Louis's life was plagued by health problems. He suffered from respiratory issues, likely exacerbated by the damp and unhealthy conditions at the Institute. His health continued to decline, and he contracted tuberculosis in the 1830s. Despite his illness, Louis continued to work tirelessly, both as a teacher at the Institute and in promoting his system of reading and writing for the blind.

Louis Braille died on 6 January 1852 at the age of 43. At the time of his death, his system was not widely adopted, but his legacy would soon be recognised. In the years following his death, the Braille system gained widespread acceptance and became the standard method of reading and writing for the blind. It transformed the lives of countless individuals, providing them with greater independence and access to education and information.

The Braille system is now used worldwide and has been adapted to almost every language. It has had a profound impact on the lives of blind individuals, enabling them to read, write, and communicate effectively. Louis Braille's invention remains one of the most significant contributions to the field of education for the blind and visually impaired.

In recognition of his contributions, Louis Braille's legacy is honoured around the world. His birthplace in Coupvray has been turned into a museum, and his name is synonymous with the system he created. Braille literacy continues to be a critical tool for blind individuals, and the system is continually adapted for use with modern technology, ensuring its continued relevance in the digital age.

Louis Braille's life is a testament to the power of perseverance and innovation. Despite the immense challenges he faced, he remained dedicated to improving the lives of others through his work. His system has stood the test of time and continues to provide opportunities for education and communication for blind individuals around the world.

Henry Dunant

Henry Dunant was born on 8 May 1828 in Geneva, Switzerland, into a devout Calvinist family known for their philanthropic activities. This early exposure to humanitarianism profoundly influenced his later life. His family instilled in him the importance of helping others, a principle that guided him throughout his life. Dunant initially pursued a career in business, and by his mid-twenties, he was a successful entrepreneur. His work took him across Europe, North Africa, and the Middle East, where he gained valuable experience and broadened his perspective on global issues.

In 1859, during a business trip to Italy, Dunant found himself near the town of Solferino, where a brutal battle between the French and Austrian armies was taking place. The Battle of Solferino, fought on 24 June 1859, was a particularly bloody conflict that resulted in tens of thousands of casualties. Dunant witnessed the aftermath of the battle firsthand and was horrified by the lack of medical care and support for the wounded soldiers. The suffering he saw left a profound impact on him and sparked a determination to do something about it.

Deeply moved by what he had witnessed, Dunant decided to write a book detailing his experiences. Published in 1862, "A Memory of Solferino" vividly described the horrors of war and the dire need for organized care for the wounded, regardless of their nationality. In his book, Dunant proposed the creation of voluntary relief societies to provide neutral and impartial aid to those injured in conflicts. He also suggested the formation of an international agreement to protect medical personnel and the wounded during wartime.

The publication of "A Memory of Solferino" garnered significant attention and support from influential figures across Europe. Among those who were inspired by Dunant's ideas were Gustave Moynier, a prominent lawyer, and philanthropist, as well as other notable citizens of Geneva. Together, they formed a committee to explore Dunant's proposals further. This committee, known as the International Committee for Relief to the Wounded, held its first meeting on 17 February 1863. This meeting marked the beginning of what would later become the International Committee of the Red Cross (ICRC).

The committee organized an international conference in October 1863, inviting representatives from various countries to discuss Dunant's ideas. The conference led to the adoption of the first Geneva Convention in 1864, which established the principles of international humanitarian law. The convention outlined the neutrality and protection of medical personnel, the establishment of voluntary relief societies, and the provision of care for the wounded without discrimination. This landmark agreement laid the foundation for modern humanitarian work and significantly influenced the conduct of warfare.

Dunant's vision had become a reality, and the Red Cross movement was born. However, despite this monumental achievement, Dunant faced personal and financial difficulties. His business ventures had failed, leaving him bankrupt and disgraced in the eyes of Geneva's society. As a result, he was forced to live in poverty and obscurity for many years, moving from place to place and relying on the kindness of friends and supporters.

During this period, Dunant continued to advocate for humanitarian causes, writing and speaking about the need for international cooperation and compassion. Despite his personal hardships, he remained committed to his principles and never wavered in his dedication to alleviating human suffering. His perseverance paid off when his contributions were finally recognised.

In 1901, Henry Dunant was awarded the first Nobel Peace Prize, shared with Frédéric Passy, a French pacifist and economist. The Nobel Committee acknowledged Dunant's role in founding the Red Cross and his efforts to promote the principles of humanitarianism and international law. This recognition brought him back into the public eye and restored some measure of his former dignity.

Dunant spent his final years in the Swiss village of Heiden, where he lived in a small room at the local hospital. Despite his frail health and financial difficulties, he continued to write and correspond with supporters around the world. He remained passionate about humanitarian causes and worked tirelessly to promote peace and compassion. Henry Dunant died on 30 October 1910, at the age of 82, leaving behind a legacy that continues to inspire and guide humanitarian efforts worldwide.

The Red Cross movement, which Dunant helped to establish, has grown into one of the most important and respected humanitarian organisations in the world. The principles he championed, including neutrality, impartiality, and humanity, remain at the core of the International Red Cross and Red Crescent Movement. His vision of a world where compassion and care for those in need transcend national boundaries and political differences has had a lasting impact on global humanitarian efforts.

In addition to his work with the Red Cross, Dunant's influence extended to the development of international humanitarian law. The Geneva Conventions, which have been expanded and revised over the years, continue to provide the legal framework for the protection of victims of armed conflict. These conventions are a testament to Dunant's enduring legacy and the profound impact of his ideas on the conduct of war and the treatment of those affected by it.

Henry Dunant's life is a powerful example of how one individual's compassion and determination can change the world. Despite facing significant personal and financial challenges, he remained steadfast in his commitment to helping others and promoting the principles of humanitarianism. His work has saved countless lives and alleviated suffering on a global scale, making him a true pioneer in the field of humanitarian aid.

Today, the Red Cross and Red Crescent Movement operates in nearly every country, providing emergency assistance, disaster relief, and education in communities affected by conflict and natural disasters. The principles and values that Henry Dunant advocated for continue to guide the work of millions of volunteers and professionals dedicated to helping those in need. His legacy lives on through their efforts and the continued impact of the organisations he helped to create.

Henry Dunant's story is a testament to the power of empathy, resilience, and the belief that one person can make a difference. His vision and dedication have left an indelible mark on the world, shaping the way we respond to human suffering and inspiring generations of humanitarians to follow in his footsteps. His contributions to the field of humanitarian aid and international law have had a lasting and profound impact, ensuring hat his legacy will be remembered and honoured for years to come.

John Logie Baird

John Logie Baird was born on 14 August 1888 in Helensburgh, Scotland, a small town on the west coast. His father, John Baird, was a clergyman, and his mother, Jessie Morrison Inglis, came from a family involved in shipbuilding. Growing up, Baird was fascinated by electronics and mechanics, often conducting experiments in his home. Despite his frequent illnesses and frail health, his curiosity and determination remained undeterred. Baird attended Larchfield Academy in Helensburgh before studying at the University of Glasgow, where he focused on electrical engineering. However, his studies were interrupted by World War I.

During the war, Baird attempted to enlist in the army but was deemed unfit for service due to his poor health. Instead, he contributed to the war effort by working on various engineering projects, including developing a system to detect submarines. After the war, he moved to the south coast of England and engaged in several business ventures, none of which were successful. His interest in television began to intensify during this period, driven by his passion for inventing and a belief in the potential of transmitting moving images electronically.

In 1923, Baird moved to Hastings, where he made significant progress on his television experiments. Working in makeshift laboratories with limited resources, he managed to create the first working television set using everyday objects such as a tea chest, biscuit tin, and bicycle lamps. Despite numerous technical challenges and frequent setbacks, his perseverance paid off. In 1924, he transmitted the first flickering image across a few feet in his lab, demonstrating the feasibility of his ideas.

Baird's breakthrough came in 1925 when he successfully transmitted the first television picture with a greyscale image. He showcased his invention to the public in Selfridge's department store in London, where he demonstrated live television transmission to a fascinated audience. This demonstration marked a significant milestone in the development of television technology and established Baird as a pioneer in the field.

In January 1926, Baird gave the world's first public demonstration of a working television system before members of the Royal Institution and a journalist from The Times. This historic event took place in his laboratory at 22 Frith Street, Soho, London. He demonstrated live moving images and explained the principles behind his invention. This demonstration was a turning point, proving that television was not just a theoretical concept but a practical technology with immense potential.

Following this success, Baird continued to refine his system. He developed the first colour television transmission using a system that involved a disc with three spirals of apertures, each transmitting a primary colour. In 1928, he achieved the first transatlantic television transmission from London to New York, demonstrating the capability of his system to transmit images over long distances. This achievement underscored the potential for television to become a global medium of communication.

Baird also pioneered other groundbreaking innovations in television technology. He developed the first video recording device, called the Phonovision, which recorded television images onto phonograph records. Although these early recordings were of limited quality, they laid the groundwork for future developments in video recording technology. Baird's inventive mind continued to explore the possibilities of television, leading him to create the first television programme for the BBC in 1929, which included a mix of news, drama, and music.

In the 1930s, Baird's electromechanical system faced competition from all-electronic television systems, particularly those developed by Marconi-EMI. Despite the technical advantages of electronic systems, Baird continued to innovate, demonstrating stereoscopic (3D) television and high-definition colour television using cathode-ray tubes. However, the BBC ultimately adopted the electronic system for its television broadcasts, leading to a decline in Baird's influence in the television industry.

During World War II, Baird's work on television was largely put on hold, but he continued to innovate in related fields. He developed a radar system and worked on various secret projects for the British government. Despite the interruption caused by the war, Baird's contributions to television continued to be recognised. After the war, he resumed his work on colour and stereoscopic television, demonstrating his continued commitment to advancing the technology.

Baird's health, which had been fragile throughout his life, began to decline further in the late 1940s. Despite this, he remained active in his research and continued to make contributions to the field of television. He moved to Bexhill-on-Sea on the south coast of England, where he lived until his death on 14 June 1946. His passing marked the end of an era for one of the most innovative minds in the history of television.

John Logie Baird's legacy is profound and far-reaching. His pioneering work laid the foundation for the modern television industry and transformed the way people consume information and entertainment. His inventions and innovations, from the first practical television system to early colour and 3D television, demonstrated his visionary understanding of the potential of this technology. Baird's contributions to television were recognised posthumously, and he is remembered as one of the great inventors of the 20th century.

The impact of Baird's work extends beyond his technical achievements. He demonstrated the power of perseverance and ingenuity, overcoming numerous obstacles and setbacks to realise his vision. His story is a testament to the importance of creativity and determination in the face of adversity. Today, his legacy is honoured in various ways, including the John Logie Baird Awards, which celebrate innovation in science and technology, and the preservation of his early television recordings, which provide a fascinating glimpse into the history of this transformative medium.

John Logie Baird's contributions to the development of television have left an indelible mark on the world. His pioneering spirit and innovative mind opened the door to a new era of communication and entertainment, fundamentally changing the way people interact with the world around them. Through his tireless work and groundbreaking inventions, Baird ensured that his name would be remembered as a true pioneer in the field of television. His legacy continues to inspire future generations of inventors and engineers, encouraging them to push the boundaries of what is possible and to imagine a better, more connected world.

Grace Hopper

Grace Hopper, born Grace Brewster Murray on December 9, 1906, in New York City, was a pioneering computer scientist and United States Navy rear admiral. From a young age, she exhibited a keen intellect and an insatiable curiosity. She was the eldest of three children and was particularly close to her father, Walter Fletcher Murray, who encouraged her interest in mathematics and science. Grace attended private schools in New York, excelling in her studies. Her academic prowess earned her a place at Vassar College, where she graduated Phi Beta Kappa with a bachelor's degree in mathematics and physics in 1928. She continued her education at Yale University, earning a master's degree in 1930 and a Ph.D. in mathematics in 1934.

Grace began her career as an educator, teaching mathematics at Vassar College. Her academic career was flourishing, but the onset of World War II changed her trajectory. In 1943, driven by a desire to serve her country, she joined the United States Naval Reserve, later known as the Women Accepted for Volunteer Emergency Service (WAVES). Despite being initially rejected due to her age and small stature, she persisted and was eventually commissioned as a lieutenant junior grade. She was assigned to the Bureau of Ordnance Computation Project at Harvard University, where she worked on the Mark I, an early electromechanical computer.

At Harvard, Hopper quickly distinguished herself. She was instrumental in programming the Mark I and authored a comprehensive 500-page manual on its operation. Her work on the Mark I laid the groundwork for her future contributions to computing. Hopper's ability to solve complex problems and her innovative thinking made her an invaluable asset. She remained at Harvard until 1949, working on the Mark II and Mark III computers.

In 1949, Hopper joined the Eckert-Mauchly Computer Corporation, where she worked on the UNIVAC I, the first commercial electronic computer. It was here that she made one of her most significant contributions to computing: the development of the first compiler. The A-0 system, developed in 1952, translated mathematical code into machine code, revolutionising the way computers were programmed. The compiler allowed programmers to use more human-readable instructions, paving the way for modern programming languages.

Hopper's work on compilers culminated in the creation of the FLOW-MATIC programming language, which was used for business applications. FLOW-MATIC influenced the development of COBOL (Common Business-Oriented Language), a high-level programming language designed for business data processing. Hopper was a driving force behind COBOL, advocating for its standardisation and adoption across different computer systems. COBOL became one of the most widely used programming languages, and Hopper's work earned her the moniker "Grandma COBOL."

Throughout her career, Hopper was known for her practical approach to problem-solving and her ability to communicate complex ideas clearly. She was a firm believer in the potential of computers to transform industries and improve efficiency. Her vision and tenacity were instrumental in advancing the field of computer science. She often challenged the status quo, famously stating, "The most damaging phrase in the language is: 'It's always been done that way.'"

In 1967, Hopper retired from the Naval Reserve with the rank of commander, but her retirement was short-lived. She was recalled to active duty in 1967 to help standardise the Navy's computer programming languages. She remained in the Navy until her final retirement in 1986, achieving the rank of rear admiral, one of the highest ranks for a woman in the Navy at that time. Hopper's work in the Navy was pivotal in modernising its computing systems and improving interoperability across different platforms.

Hopper's influence extended beyond her technical achievements. She was a passionate advocate for computer education and was dedicated to inspiring the next generation of computer scientists. She often spoke at conferences, universities, and schools, encouraging young people, especially women, to pursue careers in technology. Her charismatic personality and engaging speaking style made her a beloved figure in the tech community.

One of Hopper's most famous anecdotes involves the term "debugging." While working on the Mark II, her team discovered a moth stuck in a relay, which was causing a malfunction. They removed the moth and taped it into the logbook with the note "First actual case of bug being found." This story, though apocryphal, highlights Hopper's sense of humour and her ability to make complex concepts accessible and relatable.

Hopper received numerous accolades and honours throughout her career. She was awarded the National Medal of Technology in 1991, becoming the first female individual recipient of this prestigious award. In 2016, she was posthumously awarded the Presidential Medal of Freedom, the highest civilian honour in the United States. Her legacy is also commemorated in various ways, including the annual Grace Hopper Celebration of Women in Computing, the largest gathering of women technologists in the world.

Grace Hopper's contributions to computer science and her trailblazing career continue to inspire and influence the field. Her work laid the foundations for modern programming and established standards that are still in use today. She was a visionary who foresaw the transformative power of computers and dedicated her life to making that vision a reality. Hopper's impact is evident in the widespread use of COBOL, the principles of compiler design, and the ongoing efforts to increase diversity in technology.

Hopper's life was characterised by her relentless curiosity, her pioneering spirit, and her commitment to education and innovation. She was not only a brilliant scientist but also a mentor, a leader, and a role model for countless individuals. Her ability to bridge the gap between theoretical concepts and practical applications was instrumental in the evolution of computing. Her legacy endures through the many lives she touched, the technologies she helped create, and the continued recognition of her contributions to the field of computer science.

Grace Hopper's story is a testament to the power of perseverance, creativity, and the importance of challenging conventions. Her achievements demonstrate the impact one person can have on an entire industry and highlight the value of diversity and inclusion in driving innovation. Through her work, Hopper transformed the way we interact with technology and left an indelible mark on the world. Her legacy continues to inspire future generations to push the boundaries of what is possible and to pursue their passions with determination and courage.

Katherine Johnson

Katherine Johnson was born on 26 August 1918, in White Sulphur Springs, West Virginia. Her intelligence and talent for mathematics became evident at an early age. Her parents, Joshua and Joylette Coleman, nurtured her academic abilities, and by the time she was ten years old, Katherine had started high school. This was an extraordinary achievement, given the era and the segregationist policies that often limited educational opportunities for African Americans.

After completing high school at fourteen, Katherine attended West Virginia State College, a historically black college. There, she was mentored by Dr. William W. Schieffelin Claytor, a prominent African-American mathematician, who encouraged her to pursue a career in research mathematics. Katherine graduated summa cum laude in 1937, with degrees in mathematics and French. Her thirst for knowledge led her to become one of the first three African-American students to integrate West Virginia University's graduate school in 1939, although she left to start a family with her husband, James Goble.

In 1953, Katherine joined the National Advisory Committee for Aeronautics (NACA), which later became NASA, as a research mathematician. She began working at the Langley Research Center in Hampton, Virginia. Katherine was part of a team known as the "computers," women who performed complex calculations. Initially, she worked in the segregated West Area Computing section, but her exceptional skills soon saw her transferred to the Flight Research Division.

Katherine's first major accomplishment came during her work on the trajectory analysis for Alan Shepard's 1961 mission, Freedom 7, the first American manned flight. Her calculations were critical to the success of the mission, ensuring that Shepard's spacecraft could be accurately tracked and safely recovered. This work marked the beginning of her significant contributions to America's space programme.

As the space race heated up, Katherine's expertise became indispensable. She co-authored a paper on orbital flight, marking one of the first times a woman in her division received credit as an author of a research report. Her understanding of complex mathematical concepts and her ability to apply them to real-world problems made her an invaluable asset to NASA. Katherine's work helped lay the groundwork for future space missions, including John Glenn's orbital flight in 1962.

John Glenn, an astronaut preparing for his mission, insisted that Katherine recheck the calculations made by the newly installed electronic computers. "If she says they're good, then I'm ready to go," Glenn famously said, highlighting the trust and respect she had earned from her colleagues. Katherine confirmed the calculations, and Glenn's flight was a historic success, making him the first American to orbit the Earth.

Katherine continued to break barriers throughout her career. She worked on the Apollo programme, calculating the trajectory for the Apollo 11 mission in 1969, which landed the first humans on the Moon. Her work ensured that the lunar module would be able to rendezvous with the command module in lunar orbit, a critical element of the mission's success. Katherine's contributions were instrumental in the safe return of the Apollo 13 astronauts after their spacecraft experienced a critical failure. Her calculations helped to chart a safe path back to Earth, proving her exceptional problem-solving abilities under pressure.

Beyond her technical contributions, Katherine Johnson played a vital role in advocating for women and African Americans in science and engineering. Her career at NASA spanned over three decades, during which she shattered countless racial and gender barriers. She retired from NASA in 1986, having spent 33 years making significant contributions to aeronautics and astronautics.

Katherine's legacy extends far beyond her groundbreaking work at NASA. Her story became widely known through the book "Hidden Figures" by Margot Lee Shetterly and its subsequent film adaptation. These works brought to light the crucial roles played by Katherine and her colleagues, Dorothy Vaughan and Mary Jackson, in the success of the U.S. space programme. The recognition of their contributions inspired many, highlighting the importance of diversity and inclusion in STEM fields.

Throughout her life, Katherine received numerous awards and honours. In 2015, President Barack Obama awarded her the Presidential Medal of Freedom, the highest civilian honour in the United States, recognising her pioneering contributions to space exploration and her role as a trailblazer for women and African Americans in STEM. She was also inducted into the National Women's Hall of Fame in 2021.

Katherine Johnson's remarkable career is a testament to her extraordinary talent, perseverance, and dedication. Her work not only helped to define the trajectory of the U.S. space programme but also paved the way for future generations of women and minorities in science and technology. Her calculations and analytical prowess were crucial to some of the most significant achievements in space exploration, and her legacy continues to inspire countless individuals around the world.

Her story serves as a powerful reminder of the importance of intellectual curiosity, hard work, and the courage to overcome societal barriers. Katherine Johnson's life and achievements exemplify the impact that one individual can have on advancing human knowledge and exploration. Her contributions to NASA and her role as a pioneer for women and African Americans in STEM fields ensure that her legacy will endure for generations to come.

Emmeline Pankhurst

Emmeline Pankhurst, born Emmeline Goulden on 15 July 1858 in Manchester, England, was a central figure in the British suffragette movement. Her parents, Robert and Sophia Goulden, were politically active and staunch advocates for women's rights, which profoundly influenced Emmeline from an early age. She was introduced to the suffrage movement at fourteen after attending a women's rights meeting with her mother. This early exposure ignited her lifelong passion for gender equality.

In 1879, Emmeline married Richard Pankhurst, a barrister known for his radical views on women's rights, including supporting women's suffrage. Richard drafted the first women's suffrage bill in Britain, which, although unsuccessful, showcased his commitment to the cause. Together, Emmeline and Richard had five children, all of whom would later become involved in the suffrage movement. The Pankhurst household was a hotbed of political discussion and activism, with Emmeline at the heart of these activities, balancing her family responsibilities with her burgeoning role in the women's suffrage movement.

In 1889, Emmeline founded the Women's Franchise League, which aimed to secure the right to vote for married women. Although the league had limited success, it marked Emmeline's first formal foray into political activism. After Richard's death in 1898, Emmeline's commitment to the suffrage cause intensified. In 1903, she founded the Women's Social and Political Union (WSPU), an organisation dedicated to securing voting rights for women through militant and confrontational tactics. The WSPU's motto, "Deeds, not words," encapsulated their approach to activism, which included protests, civil disobedience, and even hunger strikes.

The WSPU, under Emmeline's leadership, quickly became known for its bold and often controversial tactics. Members disrupted political meetings, chained themselves to railings, and committed acts of arson and vandalism to draw attention to their cause. These actions often led to arrests and imprisonment. Emmeline herself was arrested numerous times and endured harsh conditions in prison, including force-feeding during hunger strikes. These sacrifices, however, only strengthened her resolve and drew public attention to the suffrage movement.

Emmeline's daughters, particularly Christabel and Sylvia, played significant roles in the WSPU. Christabel, Emmeline's eldest daughter, was a driving force behind the militant strategies, while Sylvia focused on broader social issues, leading to ideological clashes within the family and the movement. Despite these internal conflicts, the WSPU continued its relentless campaign for women's suffrage.

World War I brought a temporary halt to the WSPU's militant activities. Emmeline, demonstrating her patriotism, redirected her efforts towards supporting the war effort. She encouraged women to contribute to the war effort by taking on roles traditionally held by men, thereby proving their capability and worthiness of the vote. Emmeline's support for the war earned her respect and helped shift public opinion towards favouring women's suffrage.

In 1918, the Representation of the People Act was passed, granting voting rights to women over the age of 30 who met minimum property qualifications. Although this fell short of the WSPU's goal of universal suffrage, it was a significant victory. Emmeline continued to campaign for full voting rights until 1928, when the Equal Franchise Act was passed, granting women the right to vote on equal terms with men.

After the war, Emmeline's political focus shifted. She joined the Conservative Party and ran for Parliament, though she was not elected. She also travelled extensively, lecturing on women's rights and social reform. Emmeline's later years were marked by her declining health and the financial difficulties she faced. Despite these challenges, she remained a passionate advocate for women's rights until her death on 14 June 1928, just weeks before the passage of the Equal Franchise Act.

Emmeline Pankhurst's legacy is one of determination, resilience, and unwavering commitment to gender equality. Her leadership in the suffragette movement played a crucial role in securing voting rights for women in Britain. Her tactics, though often controversial, were instrumental in drawing attention to the cause and achieving significant legal reforms. Emmeline's life and work continue to inspire generations of activists and feminists around the world, reminding us of the power of dedicated and fearless advocacy in the pursuit of justice and equality.

Mikhail Gorbachev

Mikhail Gorbachev was born on 2 March 1931, in Privolnoye, a small village in the Stavropol region of southern Russia. His early life was marked by the hardships of rural Soviet existence, particularly during the turmoil of World War II and the German occupation. Gorbachev's parents, Sergei and Maria, were peasants, and his father was a combine harvester operator. Despite the challenging conditions, Gorbachev excelled in school, demonstrating a keen intellect and a strong work ethic, traits that would later define his political career.

In 1950, Gorbachev enrolled at Moscow State University, where he studied law. During his time at university, he joined the Communist Party of the Soviet Union (CPSU) and met his future wife, Raisa Titarenko, who was studying sociology. Raisa would become a significant influence and support throughout his life. Gorbachev graduated in 1955 and returned to Stavropol, where he began his political career in the Komsomol, the Communist Party's youth organisation.

Gorbachev quickly rose through the ranks of the regional party structure, demonstrating an aptitude for leadership and a commitment to reform. His rise was marked by a series of increasingly prominent positions within the party. By 1970, he had become the First Secretary of the Stavropol Regional Committee, effectively the head of the Stavropol region. During his tenure, Gorbachev focused on improving agricultural productivity and living standards, gaining a reputation as a pragmatic and effective leader.

In 1978, Gorbachev was appointed to the Central Committee's Secretariat, and in 1979, he joined the Politburo, the highest decision-making body in the Soviet Union. His promotion to the Politburo marked the beginning of his influence on national policy. Gorbachev was a protégé of Yuri Andropov, who served as General Secretary of the CPSU from 1982 to 1984. Andropov recognised Gorbachev's potential and supported his rise within the party.

In March 1985, following the death of General Secretary Konstantin Chernenko, Gorbachev was elected as the General Secretary of the CPSU, the highest position in the Soviet Union. At the age of 54, he was one of the youngest leaders in Soviet history and brought a new energy and vision to the leadership. Gorbachev inherited a country burdened by economic stagnation, political corruption, and a costly arms race with the United States.

Gorbachev introduced a series of sweeping reforms aimed at revitalising the Soviet economy and society. His policies of glasnost (openness) and perestroika (restructuring) were designed to promote greater transparency, reduce corruption, and introduce elements of market economics. Glasnost allowed for increased freedom of speech, a freer press, and more open discussion of political and social issues. Perestroika sought to decentralise economic control, reduce the role of central planning, and encourage private enterprise.

These reforms were met with mixed reactions within the Soviet Union. While many welcomed the increased freedoms and opportunities, others resisted the changes, fearing the loss of their privileges and the potential for instability. Gorbachev's policies also had significant international implications, as they led to a reduction in Cold War tensions. He pursued détente with the West, engaging in arms control negotiations with the United States. In 1987, Gorbachev and U.S. President Ronald Reagan signed the Intermediate-Range Nuclear Forces (INF) Treaty, which eliminated an entire class of nuclear weapons.

Gorbachev's foreign policy, known as the "new thinking," advocated for the end of the ideological conflict between East and West and sought cooperation on global issues such as disarmament, environmental protection, and economic development. His willingness to reduce the Soviet military presence in Eastern Europe and his support for non-intervention in the internal affairs of other countries had profound consequences. In 1989, a wave of revolutions swept through Eastern Europe, leading to the fall of communist regimes and the eventual dismantling of the Iron Curtain.

The most dramatic moment of Gorbachev's tenure came with the fall of the Berlin Wall in November 1989. This event symbolised the end of the Cold War and the reunification of Germany. Gorbachev's decision not to intervene militarily in Eastern Europe earned him international acclaim but also criticism from hardliners within the Soviet Union who saw it as a betrayal of Soviet interests.

Domestically, Gorbachev's reforms led to increased political pluralism and the introduction of multi-candidate elections. In 1988, the Soviet Union held its first competitive elections since the 1920s for the newly created Congress of People's Deputies. These elections allowed for a broader representation of views and were a significant step towards political liberalisation. However, the rapid pace of change also unleashed ethnic tensions and nationalist movements within the Soviet republics, challenging the unity of the Soviet state.

By 1990, the Soviet Union was facing severe economic difficulties, with shortages of goods, declining industrial output, and rising inflation. Gorbachev's attempts to implement more radical economic reforms were met with resistance from both conservatives and radicals, leading to a political stalemate. In August 1991, a group of hardline Communist officials attempted a coup to remove Gorbachev from power. The coup failed, largely due to the resistance led by Boris Yeltsin, the President of the Russian Soviet Federative Socialist Republic. However, the coup further weakened Gorbachev's authority and accelerated the dissolution of the Soviet Union.

In December 1991, the leaders of Russia, Ukraine, and Belarus signed the Belavezha Accords, declaring the Soviet Union dissolved and establishing the Commonwealth of Independent States (CIS). Gorbachev resigned as President of the Soviet Union on 25 December 1991, marking the end of the Soviet state. His resignation speech reflected his deep disappointment at the collapse of the Soviet Union but also his pride in the democratic and peaceful changes that had taken place.

After his resignation, Gorbachev remained active in international affairs, promoting democratic governance, disarmament, and environmental sustainability. He established the Gorbachev Foundation, which focused on research and policy advocacy, and the Green Cross International, an environmental organisation. Gorbachev continued to write and lecture on global issues, sharing his experiences and insights on the challenges facing the world.

Gorbachev's legacy is complex and often contested. He is widely praised in the West for his role in ending the Cold War and reducing the threat of nuclear conflict. His commitment to glasnost and perestroika helped to transform the Soviet Union and set the stage for the emergence of democratic governance in Russia and other former Soviet republics. However, within Russia, opinions are more divided. Some view him as a visionary leader who brought necessary reforms and freedoms, while others blame him for the economic hardships and the loss of Soviet power and prestige.

Throughout his life, Gorbachev demonstrated a remarkable capacity for leadership, a commitment to reform, and a vision for a more open and cooperative world. His efforts to promote dialogue, reduce tensions, and advocate for a better future continue to resonate. Mikhail Gorbachev's contributions to global peace and his transformative impact on the Soviet Union and the world will be remembered as pivotal moments in the history of the 20th century. His death on 30 August 2022 marked the passing of one of the most influential figures in modern history.

Rachel Carson

Rachel Carson was born on 27 May 1907, in Springdale, Pennsylvania. She was the youngest of three children and grew up on a small family farm, where she developed a deep love for nature. Her mother, Maria McLean Carson, encouraged her interest in the natural world, fostering a curiosity that would shape her future. Carson's early experiences exploring the forests and streams around her home cultivated a lifelong passion for the environment.

Carson's academic journey began with her enrolment at the Pennsylvania College for Women, now Chatham University, where she initially studied English before switching to biology. She graduated in 1929 and went on to pursue a master's degree in zoology at Johns Hopkins University. Despite facing financial difficulties during the Great Depression, Carson excelled in her studies, demonstrating an exceptional aptitude for science and a talent for writing.

After completing her master's degree, Carson briefly worked as a teacher and later joined the U.S. Bureau of Fisheries in 1936, where she wrote radio scripts and pamphlets. Her ability to convey complex scientific concepts to the public was soon recognised, and she began writing articles for newspapers and magazines. This work laid the foundation for her future career as a writer and environmental advocate.

In 1941, Carson published her first book, "Under the Sea-Wind," which presented marine biology in a way that was accessible to general readers. Although it received positive reviews, the book did not sell well initially due to the onset of World War II. However, it established Carson's reputation as a talented writer capable of merging scientific knowledge with lyrical prose.

Carson's breakthrough came with her second book, "The Sea Around Us," published in 1951. The book became an immediate bestseller, winning the National Book Award and remaining on the New York Times bestseller list for 86 weeks. "The Sea Around Us" explored the history and science of the oceans, capturing the imagination of readers with its vivid descriptions and engaging narrative. This success allowed Carson to resign from her job at the U.S. Fish and Wildlife Service, where she had been promoted to editor-in-chief of publications, and devote herself to writing full-time.

Following the success of "The Sea Around Us," Carson published "The Edge of the Sea" in 1955, completing her trilogy on marine life. Each of these works reflected her deep knowledge of marine biology and her ability to communicate scientific concepts to a broad audience. Through her books, Carson aimed to foster a greater appreciation for the natural world and to highlight the interconnectedness of all living things.

Carson's most influential work, "Silent Spring," was published in 1962. This groundbreaking book exposed the environmental dangers of indiscriminate pesticide use, particularly focusing on the adverse effects of DDT. Carson meticulously documented the harm that pesticides were causing to wildlife, the environment, and human health. "Silent Spring" challenged the practices of agricultural scientists and the chemical industry, calling for a change in the way humans viewed and interacted with the natural world.

The publication of "Silent Spring" sparked widespread public concern and debate. Carson faced significant opposition from the chemical industry, which sought to discredit her work and undermine her credibility. Despite these attacks, "Silent Spring" gained support from the scientific community and the general public. The book's impact was profound, leading to a greater awareness of environmental issues and contributing to the rise of the modern environmental movement.

'Silent Spring' played a crucial role in the establishment of regulatory policies governing pesticide use. It led to the eventual ban on DDT in the United States and the creation of the Environmental Protection Agency (EPA) in 1970. Carson's work underscored the need for science-based regulation and greater oversight of chemical substances to protect human health and the environment.

Throughout her career, Carson remained committed to her vision of a harmonious relationship between humans and nature. She continued to write and speak about environmental issues, advocating for conservation and sustainable practices. Her eloquence and conviction inspired a generation of environmental activists and helped to shift public attitudes towards greater environmental stewardship.

Carson's personal life was marked by her dedication to her family and her work. She faced significant health challenges, including a battle with breast cancer that ultimately led to her death on 14 April 1964. Despite her illness, Carson continued to work on her writing and advocacy, leaving behind a legacy that continues to influence environmental policy and thought.

Carson's contributions to environmental science and her role in raising awareness about the ecological impacts of human activities have been widely recognised. She received numerous honours and awards, including posthumous induction into the National Women's Hall of Fame and the establishment of the Rachel Carson Wildlife Refuge in Maine. Her work has inspired countless individuals to pursue careers in environmental science and to advocate for the protection of the natural world.

Rachel Carson's life and achievements exemplify the power of science communication and the importance of advocacy in effecting social and environmental change. Her ability to translate complex scientific concepts into compelling narratives helped to bridge the gap between scientists and the public, fostering a greater understanding of and appreciation for the natural world. Carson's legacy is a testament to the impact that one individual can have in raising awareness and driving progress towards a more sustainable future.

Her pioneering work laid the foundation for the modern environmental movement and continues to inspire efforts to protect and preserve the natural world. Carson's call for a balanced and respectful relationship with nature remains as relevant today as it was during her lifetime, serving as a guiding principle for environmental advocates and policymakers around the world.

Steve Jobs

Steve Jobs was born on 24 February 1955 in San Francisco, California, to two university students who put him up for adoption. He was adopted by Paul and Clara Jobs, who raised him in Silicon Valley. Growing up, Jobs showed an early interest in electronics and engineering, influenced by his adoptive father, who taught him how to take apart and rebuild electronics in their garage. This hands-on experience nurtured his technical skills and fascination with innovative technology.

Jobs attended Homestead High School in Cupertino, where he became friends with Steve Wozniak, an electronics whiz. After high school, Jobs enrolled at Reed College in Portland, Oregon, but dropped out after six months, although he continued to audit classes that interested him, such as calligraphy. This seemingly inconsequential interest later influenced the design of the Macintosh computer's typography.

In 1974, Jobs returned to California and joined Atari as a video game designer. Seeking spiritual enlightenment, he left Atari to travel to India, where he explored Eastern philosophies and practices. Upon his return to the U.S., Jobs reconnected with Wozniak, who had been working on a personal computer. Recognising the commercial potential of Wozniak's creation, Jobs convinced him to form a partnership. In 1976, they founded Apple Computer, Inc., along with Ronald Wayne.

Their first product, the Apple I, was sold as a motherboard, lacking a keyboard or monitor. Despite its rudimentary nature, it was a success among hobbyists. The following year, they launched the Apple II, which was a breakthrough in personal computing. The Apple II featured a colour display, an integrated keyboard, and expandable memory, becoming one of the first highly successful mass-produced microcomputers.

Apple's success continued to grow, and in 1980, the company went public, making Jobs a millionaire. He then focused on developing the Macintosh, introduced in 1984. The Macintosh was notable for its graphical user interface, which was more user-friendly than the text-based interfaces of other computers at the time. This innovation set a new standard for personal computing, but despite its technical achievements, the Macintosh initially struggled in the market.

Internal tensions within Apple led to a power struggle, and in 1985, Jobs was ousted from the company he co-founded. Undeterred, he founded NeXT Inc., aiming to create powerful workstations for the higher-education and business markets. While NeXT computers were technologically advanced, featuring innovations such as an object-oriented software development system, they were commercially unsuccessful due to their high cost.

Simultaneously, Jobs acquired The Graphics Group (later renamed Pixar) from Lucasfilm in 1986. Pixar initially focused on creating high-end graphics computers, but pivoted to animation, producing groundbreaking films such as "Toy Story" in 1995, the first entirely computer-animated feature film. Pixar's success was monumental, eventually leading to its acquisition by Disney in 2006, with Jobs becoming Disney's largest individual shareholder.

In 1996, Apple acquired NeXT, bringing Jobs back to the company. He returned as interim CEO in 1997, quickly revitalising the struggling company with a series of strategic moves and innovative products. He streamlined Apple's product line, eliminating poorly performing products, and focused on the development of new, groundbreaking products.

In 1998, Apple introduced the iMac, an all-in-one computer known for its distinctive design and ease of use. The iMac was a commercial success and signalled the beginning of Apple's resurgence. Jobs's focus on design, simplicity, and user experience became hallmarks of Apple's products. He fostered a culture of innovation, pushing the boundaries of technology and design.

Under Jobs's leadership, Apple launched a series of revolutionary products that transformed the technology industry. The iPod, introduced in 2001, revolutionised the music industry by allowing users to store and play thousands of songs on a portable device. The iTunes Store, launched in 2003, provided a legal platform for music downloads, changing the way people purchased and consumed music.

In 2007, Apple entered the mobile phone market with the iPhone, a device that combined a phone, an iPod, and an internet communicator. The iPhone's touch screen interface and app ecosystem redefined the smartphone industry and positioned Apple as a leader in mobile technology. The App Store, launched in 2008, created a new economy for software developers and expanded the functionality of the iPhone.

Jobs continued to innovate with the introduction of the iPad in 2010, a tablet computer that bridged the gap between smartphones and laptops. The iPad's success further cemented Apple's position as a leading technology company. Jobs's ability to anticipate market trends and his relentless pursuit of excellence were key factors in Apple's success.

Despite his professional achievements, Jobs faced significant health challenges. He was diagnosed with a rare form of pancreatic cancer in 2003. Though he initially responded to treatment and continued to work, his health issues persisted. In 2009, Jobs took a leave of absence for a liver transplant, returning to work later that year. However, his health continued to decline, leading to another medical leave in 2011. In August 2011, Jobs resigned as CEO of Apple, handing over the reins to Tim Cook, though he remained involved with the company as chairman of the board.

Steve Jobs passed away on 5 October 2011, at the age of 56. His death was met with an outpouring of grief from around the world. Jobs was remembered not only for his technological innovations but also for his visionary leadership and ability to inspire. His legacy is evident in the continued success of Apple, which remains one of the most valuable companies in the world.

Jobs's impact extends beyond his products. He revolutionised multiple industries, from personal computing and animated films to music, phones, and tablet computing. His emphasis on design and user experience set new standards, influencing countless products and companies. Jobs's ability to anticipate and create demand for new products reshaped consumer technology and changed the way people interact with digital devices.

Steve Jobs's life was marked by a relentless pursuit of innovation and a passion for perfection. His contributions to technology and design have left an indelible mark on the world, and his vision continues to inspire future generations of entrepreneurs, designers, and engineers. Jobs's story is a testament to the power of creativity, determination, and the belief that technology can change the world.

Malala Yousafzai

Malala Yousafzai was born on 12 July 1997 in Mingora, a town in the Swat District of Pakistan's Khyber Pakhtunkhwa province. Her father, Ziauddin Yousafzai, was an educator and ran a chain of schools known as the Khushal Public School. He was a passionate advocate for education, particularly for girls, in a region where the Taliban frequently targeted female education. From an early age, Malala was influenced by her father's activism and developed a keen interest in learning and advocating for girls' right to education.

Malala's journey into the global spotlight began when she was just eleven years old. In 2008, the Taliban took control of Swat Valley and banned girls from attending school. Malala, determined to continue her education, began writing a blog under the pseudonym Gul Makai for the BBC Urdu service. In her blog, she detailed her life under Taliban rule and the challenges she and other girls faced in pursuing an education. Her poignant and courageous writings brought her international attention, highlighting the plight of girls in Swat Valley and other regions under Taliban influence.

As the situation in Swat Valley worsened, Malala continued to speak out, despite the growing dangers. She appeared in documentary films and gave interviews, advocating for girls' education and criticising the Taliban's oppressive regime. Her activism made her a target, but she remained undeterred. In October 2012, at the age of fifteen, Malala was shot in the head by a Taliban gunman while riding a bus home from school. The attack was an attempt to silence her and intimidate others who supported girls' education.

Malala was critically injured and airlifted to a military hospital in Peshawar before being transferred to Birmingham, England, for further treatment. The attack sparked outrage and condemnation worldwide, bringing Malala's cause to the forefront of global consciousness. Her resilience and determination to recover inspired millions, and she received extensive medical treatment, eventually making a remarkable recovery.

In the wake of the attack, Malala's advocacy for education intensified. She and her father established the Malala Fund, a non-profit organisation dedicated to promoting girls' education worldwide. The Fund aims to empower girls through education, advocating for policy changes and providing financial support to local education initiatives. Malala continued her own education in Birmingham, attending Edgbaston High School for Girls and later studying at the University of Oxford, where she earned a degree in Philosophy, Politics, and Economics.

Malala's efforts were recognised globally, and she received numerous accolades for her bravery and activism. In 2013, she co-authored the memoir "I Am Malala: The Girl Who Stood Up for Education and Was Shot by the Taliban," which became an international bestseller. The book detailed her life, her activism, and the attack that nearly took her life. It also highlighted the broader struggle for girls' education and the importance of standing up against oppression.

In 2014, at the age of seventeen, Malala became the youngest-ever recipient of the Nobel Peace Prize, sharing the award with Indian children's rights activist Kailash Satyarthi. The Nobel Committee recognised her efforts to advocate for the rights of children and education for girls, emphasising the global significance of her work. The award brought further attention to the issues Malala championed and underscored the importance of education in achieving peace and development.

Malala's activism extended beyond education, as she also became a vocal advocate for human rights, women's rights, and the plight of refugees. She used her platform to speak out against various forms of injustice and to call for greater international cooperation in addressing global challenges. Her speeches at the United Nations and other international forums resonated with audiences worldwide, inspiring a new generation of activists and leaders.

Despite the numerous accolades and widespread recognition, Malala remained grounded and committed to her cause. She continued to visit countries affected by conflict and poverty, meeting with girls and communities to understand their struggles and to advocate for their right to education. Her visits to refugee camps in Lebanon, Jordan, and Kenya highlighted the educational needs of displaced children and the importance of international support in addressing these challenges.

Malala's impact on global education policy has been profound. Her advocacy contributed to the adoption of Sustainable Development Goal 4 by the United Nations, which aims to ensure inclusive and equitable quality education and promote lifelong learning opportunities for all. She also worked with global leaders and organisations to secure funding and support for education initiatives, recognising that investment in education is crucial for sustainable development and social progress.

Malala's story has been the subject of numerous documentaries, films, and books, further amplifying her message and inspiring others to join the fight for education and equality. The 2015 documentary "He Named Me Malala" provided an intimate look at her life and activism, reaching a broad audience and raising awareness about the importance of girls' education.

Throughout her journey, Malala has faced numerous challenges and threats, but her unwavering commitment to her cause has remained a source of inspiration for millions. Her courage in the face of adversity and her ability to transform personal tragedy into a powerful force for change demonstrate the profound impact that one individual can have on the world.

Malala's legacy continues to grow as she remains an active and influential voice in the global movement for education and human rights. Her work through the Malala Fund has enabled countless girls to access education and pursue their dreams, breaking down barriers and challenging societal norms. Malala's vision of a world where every girl has the opportunity to learn and thrive is a testament to her belief in the power of education to transform lives and communities.

As she continues her advocacy, Malala's message resonates with people of all ages and backgrounds, reminding us of the importance of standing up for what is right and the transformative power of education. Her life and achievements serve as a powerful reminder that even in the face of the most daunting challenges, one person can make a significant difference and inspire others to join the fight for a more just and equitable world.

Printed in Great Britain
by Amazon